THE NAPOLEONIC LIBRARY

WATERLOO LECTURES

A STUDY OF THE CAMPAIGN OF 1815

Colonel Charles Chesney

Introduction by Peter Hofschröer

FRONTLINE BOOKS

Waterloo Lectures

A Greenhill Book

Published in 1997 by Greenhill Books, Lionel Leventhal Limited
www.greenhillbooks.com

This edition published in 2015 by

Frontline Books
an imprint of Pen & Sword Books Ltd,
47 Church Street, Barnsley, S. Yorkshire, S70 2AS
For more information on our books, please visit
www.frontline-books.com, email info@frontline-books.com
or write to us at the above address.

This edition © Lionel Leventhal Ltd, 1997
Introduction © Peter Hofschröer, 1997

ISBN: 978-1-84832-833-4

CIP data records for this title are available from the British Library

Publishing History

Waterloo Lectures was first published in 1868; revised second edition 1869; revised
third edition 1874; fourth edition reprinted exactly as the third edition in 1907
(Longman, Green and Co., London); and revised fifth edition in 1997 (Greenhill
Books). The fifth edition is now reproduced complete and unabridged.

Printed and bound by CPI Group (UK) Ltd, Croydon, CR0 4YY

CONTENTS

Map of Belgium, with French Frontier of 1815

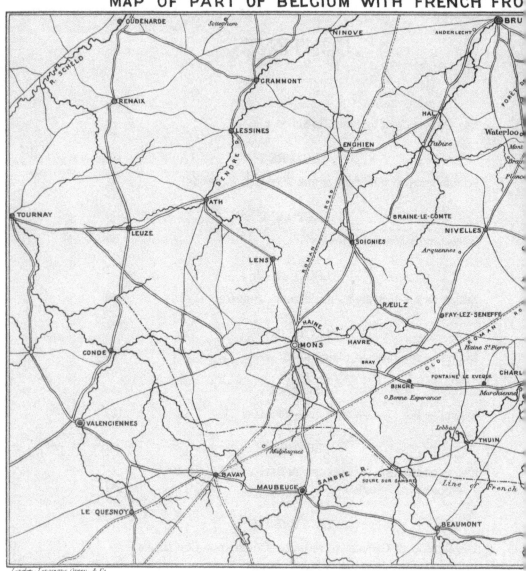

OUDENARDE
Sotteghem
NINOVE
ANDERLECHT
BRU

R. SCHELD
GRAMMONT
HAL
FORÊT D

RENAIX
LESSINES
ENGHIEN
Tubize
Waterloo
Mont
Brai
Planc

DENDRE R
ATH
BRAINE-LE-COMTE
NIVELLES

TOURNAY
LEUZE
SOIGNIES
Arquennes

LENS
ROMAN ROAD

RŒULZ
FAY-LEZ-SENEFFE

HAINE R
MONS HAVRE
ROMAN RO

CONDE
BRAY
Haine St Pierre

OLD
FONTAINE LE EVEQUE
CHARL

BINCHE
Marchienne
Bonne Esperance

VALENCIENNES
Lobbes
THUIN

Malplaquet
SAMBRE R.
Line of French

BAVAY
SOLRE SUR SAMBRE

MAUBEUGE

LE QUESNOY
BEAUMONT

London: Longmans, Green, & Co

1815 TO ILLUSTRATE CAMPAIGN OF WATERLOO

LOUVAIN

TIRLEMONT

ST TROND

TONGRES

Landen

WAVRE

Jodoigne

Dion le-Mont

Baraque

Carbaix

NIL ST VINCENT

HANNUT

LIEGE

ont St Cubert

PERWEZ

Ramillier

Sort les Walhain

Gentinnes

Grand Leez

Sauvenure

GEMBLOUX

MEUSE R.

Sombreffe

Ligny

Le Mazy

HUY

EURUS

NAMUR

SAMBRE R.

R. MEUSE

CINEY

SOSOYE

DINANT

PHILIPPEVILLE

To Giver

10   15   20

LISH MILES

List of Works and Editions chiefly used as Marginal References.

CONTRACTED AS

Müff. Hist. . . . . Müffling's History of the Campaign of 1815, translated by Sir John Sinclair (London, 1816).

Mü. Mem. . . . Müffling's Passages out of My Life, translated by Yorke (London, 1853).

Pr. Off. . . . . (Prussian Official). Recueil de Batailles (Berlin, 1821).

Claus. . . . . . Clausewitz. Feldzug von 1815 (Berlin 1835).

Ense . . . . . Varnhagen von Ense's Leben Blücher's (Berlin, 1845).

Brial. . . . . . Histoire du Duc de Wellington, par le Colonel Brialmont (Brussels, 1858).

Loben S. . . . . Van Loben Sels, Précis de la Campagne de 1815 (Hague, 1849).

Sib. . . . . . . Siborne's History of the War in the Netherlands (London, 1844).

Hamley . . . . Hamley's Wellington's Career (London, 1860).

Kenn. . . . . . Notes on Waterloo, by Sir J. Shaw Kennedy (London, 1865).

Hooper . . . . Waterloo, by G. Hooper (London, 1862).

Gur. . . . . . The Wellington Dispatches, by Gurwood.

Sup. Dis. . . . . Supplementary Dispatches of Wellington.

Doc. . . . . . Accounts and Official Documents relating to Waterloo, collected by a Near Observer (Eighth Edition, London, 1816).

Leeke . . . . . Lord Seaton's Regiment at Waterloo, by W. Leeke (London, 1866). (Used for battle only.)

Jom. . . . . . Précis de la Campagne de 1815, par le Général Jomini (Paris, 1839).

Gourg. . . . . Napoléon. Campagne de 1815, par le Général Gourgaud (London, 1818).

Mém. . . . . . Napoléon. Mémoires pour servir, &c. (Paris, 1830).

Cha. . . . . . Charras. Campagne de 1815 (Brussels, 1858).

Quin. . . . . . Quinet. Campagne de 1815 (Paris, 1862).

Thi. . . . . . Thiers. Histoire du Consulat et de l'Empire (Paris, 1862).

Mil. Woch. . . . Militair Wochenblatt (the military journal of Berlin).

Büd. . . . Professor Max Büdinger. 'Zur Waterloo-Literatur' (Leipsic, 1869).

INTRODUCTION

The publication of Waterloo literature seems to be a perennial occupation in the English-speaking world, producing a flood of literature which has not abated since those dramatic events of June 1815. However, of this great mountain of books perhaps only two works really stand out, namely those by Siborne and Chesney. Despite the unfounded criticism of the former which has appeared recently, Siborne consulted every available Allied authority on the campaign, sought personal statements from many of the leading participants, and thus made every attempt to present the facts in his narrative. Chesney, first writing two decades after Siborne, was praised for the impartiality of his *Waterloo Lectures*, a concise and most informative analysis of the campaign. As 'my country right or wrong' historians have dominated this particular aspect of European history, any attempt to establish the facts and present an objective analysis of them was indeed remarkable. These two works thus complement each other, and, at a time when most Europeans are endeavouring to put the national rivalries of the previous century or so behind them, this long overdue reprint of Chesney's work is to be welcomed.

Both Siborne's and Chesney's works were, at the time of their publication, controversial and, to an extent, revisionist history. In a post-Waterloo Britain, the great war hero the Duke of Wellington was idolised by certain sections of British society. Siborne's work did not always follow the 'official' line as given by Gleig, the Iron Duke's great admirer. Indeed, when supplied with convincing documentary evidence that conflicted with this version of events, particularly from the Prussian side, Siborne, in later editions, did not hesitate to amend his account. Chesney followed the lead given. His work ran to four editions. After it had, on the recommendation of great soldiers such as Moltke the Elder, been translated into German and French, Chesney too did not hesitate to make amendments suggested by Continental authorities in later editions, even if this conflicted with the popular accounts of those events which were becoming increasingly nationalistic.

The rise of nationalism in Britain in the latter half of the nineteenth century, and particularly after the establishment of the second German Empire, pushed historians of Chesney's calibre to one side. Those writers for whom history was the mere hand-maiden of contemporary politics came to the fore. Works such as those by Robinson and Becke were published. For such writers impartiality was a sin and documented facts might be discarded if they did not fit preconceived notions. The concept of objectivity, exemplified by Siborne and Chesney, died out in Britain and it fell to an American, John Codman Ropes, to continue it. However, two world wars resulted in a Europe divided along national lines, and a world divided by ideology. Only in recent years, thanks to the foresighted dismantling of barriers within Europe and the fall of the Iron Curtain, have the scars of the recent past begun to heal. Part of this healing process must be to go back to the scrupulous methods Siborne and Chesney when writing on the events of 1815, and to endeavour to establish the facts free from any national bias.

While Siborne's great classic has hardly ever been out of print since its first publication, the most recent edition of Chesney to date was that published in 1907. His work evidently did not meet the criteria of a public traumatised by the events of the First World War. Some ninety years later, once more this great work is at last available, to a reading public which it is to be hoped, has learned enough from the tragic events of this century to seek an account of events unblemished by national prejudice.

A nephew of General Francis Rawdon Chesney, Charles Cornwallis Chesney was born on 29th September 1826 near Kilkeel in County Down, Ireland, in his uncle's house. The Chesneys were a family with military traditions: Charles Cornwallis's father, also named Charles Cornwallis, had been a captain in the Bengal artillery of the East India Company until ill-health had forced him to return to Britain where he died in 1830.

Having lost his father when he was four years of age, Charles Cornwallis junior was brought up by his mother who was, apparently, a person of extraordinary energy and strength of character. He went on to be educated at Blundell's school in Tiverton and then for a year at a private school in Exeter before, in 1843, obtaining a nomination to the Royal Military Academy, which was then in Woolwich, and beginning a successful military career.

In 1845, Chesney was commissioned as a sub-lieutenant in the Royal Engineers, passing out as head of his term. His first posting was to Ireland, then to the Bermudas and the West Indies. Chesney returned to Britain in 1853, and was then ordered to New Zealand where, in 1854, he was placed in command of a company. However, suffering from poor health, he returned to Britain two years later.

During this early part of his military career, Chesney had been developing into a military critic of sound reputation. As such, he was offered and accepted a post of professor of military history at the Cadet College in Sandhurst, which later became the renowned Staff College. His reputation grew with this appointment, and Chesney soon came to be regarded in Britain as the leading military critic of his day.

In the first half of the nineteenth century, the formal teaching of the military sciences was relatively new in Britain and tried and tested teaching materials were hard to come by. This is where Chesney came into his element; his major achievement was to develop the methods and tools by which his students could be formally instructed. The cornerstone of Chesney's teaching method was to take the judicial approach to military criticism and establish the credibility of a witness to great military events. The basis for an impartial analysis could be established. This method is clearly illustrated throughout Chesney's writings. One could say with justification that this engineer officer was the founder of modern teaching methods for staff officers of the British army.

With a reputation for clear, logical and graceful expression, Chesney was popular with his students, and his lectures were always well attended. His first published work was *Campaigns in Virginia and Maryland* and it appeared in 1863, while the American Civil War was still in progress. It was most unusual for critical works on a war to be published before the war had ended. A second edition appeared a year later and indicates the popularity of Chesney's writings.

Waterloo Lectures, of which the fourth edition is republished here, first appeared in 1868. It soon sold out, with a further two editions being printed by 1874. Noted for its absolute impartiality, this work soon became a standard text at military schools, and was translated into French and German. Moltke the Elder, architect of Prussia's victories in the Wars of Unification (1864–1871) and regarded as one of history's greatest staff officers, was instrumental in having the work translated into German. Lettow-Vorbeck, the German staff historian who wrote an official history of the Waterloo campaign, described Chesney's account, perhaps a little unfairly, as the 'first impartial English account'. Once *Waterloo Lectures* had been published in French and German, the authorities in those countries were able to comment on this work, and make suggestions for improvements. These improvements were then incorporated in the third edition. The fourth edition was a straight reprint of the previous edition.

It is surprising that this work has not been readily available since then. It makes an excellent companion volume to Siborne's comprehensive *History of the Waterloo Campaign*, and a fine supplement to Ropes' critique which was published towards the end of the nineteenth century, and which has also recently been reprinted.

Other works by Chesney include: *The Tactical Use of Fortresses* (published in 1868), *The Military Resources of Prussia and France* (1870) and *Essays in Military Biography* (reprinted 1874), a collection of papers taken from the *Edinburgh Review*, to which Chesney was a frequent contributor, and from *Fraser's Magazine*. This particular volume included essays on the military careers of Lee and Grant, two leading generals of the then recent American Civil War.

Chesney also served as a member of the Royal Commission on Military Education which sat from 1868 to 1870. This commission was part of a general effort to reform the British army and modernise its structures at a time of great changes in the balance of power in Europe. A clear and critical mind like Chesney's was a great attribute to such a process of renewal, and he was able to make a positive contribution. After having been sent to report on the Franco-Prussian War in 1871, Chesney became closely involved with Cardwell's army reforms, and in particular with his scheme for the localisation of the army.

On his promotion to the rank of lieutenant-colonel in 1868, Chesney was posted to Aldershot. There he remained for five years before obtaining the brevet rank of colonel, after which he was appointed to command the Home District of the Royal Engineers. Sadly, this great military critic caught a chill while carrying out his duties, and died of pneumonia on 19th March 1876, at the early age of forty-nine. He was buried at Sandhurst.

The premature death of this fine officer and respected teacher represented a major loss to the writing of military history in Britain. While the general staffs of the armies of continental Europe devoted considerable resources to the production of high quality texts on earlier wars, the British army lacked such a body by which standards could be set. Chesney was a person with influence and good organisational skills; he might have been able to do much more towards the promotion of good quality military history in the late nineteenth century. However, this was not to be the case; we can only ensure that the few works he did produce are held in justifiable high regard.

Peter Hofschröer, 1997.

PREFACE

TO

THE THIRD EDITION.

———◦◦———

THE German and French translations of this work
having made it widely known upon the Continent, it
is not surprising that suggestions for corrections and
additions have reached me from various countries.
Some of these had been anticipated in the Second
Edition.   Of others it is enough to say, that the
insertion of them would have raised new controversies on unimportant questions, or added superfluous
matter to what was never designed to include every
detail of the campaign.   But there are two important
points on which some of my critics have thrown fresh
light, which it would be unjust to them not to use.

One of these concerns the alleged neglect of
Blücher to communicate to Wellington his defeat
at Ligny and consequent retreat, as soon as the
abandonment of the ground became inevitable.   The

researches made in Germany since the Official Berlin
edition of these Lectures was published, have not only
disproved this charge, but have identified the bearer
of the message (whose escort was dispersed and himself shot down by the French near Quatre Bras)
with a retired Lieutenant-Colonel Winterfeldt, who
died not long since at Hanover at the advanced age
of ninety-four. It was a positive duty to make the
necessary correction in the text, and this has been
done accordingly.

The other point relates to the question of Wellington's supposed line of retreat in case of his position
at Waterloo having been forced before the Prussians
came up. It has been usually taken for granted
that this would have lain direct to his rear through
the wood of Soignies, and much controversy has
arisen on the probable advantage or disadvantage of
such a course. But if Wellington's own statement,
deliberately made not many years after to a Dutch
officer of high rank, may be taken literally, he looked
to no such movement as advisable at the crisis of the
battle, but rather to retiring with the bulk of his
force directly towards the expected army of Blücher.
As in this view his right wing must have been left to
effect a separate retreat westward, a fair solution is

at once offered of that obstinate retention to the last
of the large detachment at Hal, on which so much
criticism has been spent.   I have not hesitated to
adopt this view, since the fact of his having contem-
plated thus retiring rests upon good evidence, due to
the researches of Professor Büdinger of Zürich, who
has paid these Lectures the compliment of making
them the text of an exhaustive study of his own on
the Literature of Waterloo.

ALDERSHOT: *March* 13, 1874.

PREFACE

THE SECOND EDITION.

————◆◇◆————

THERE is a double satisfaction in being called upon so
soon for a Second Edition of this work, inasmuch as
it is thus shown that the Author's effort to treat his
subject in an impartial spirit has met the approval of
his own countrymen, while it ' has done something '—
to use words which come from high authority—' to
heal a soreness which has been kept up among our
Waterloo Allies these fifty years, by our arrogating
to ourselves the whole credit of the victory for which
they bled as well as we.' It may be added, that
although the French reviewers not unnaturally think
the view here taken of their great soldier unduly
severe, they admit liberally that their gallant army has
suffered no injustice. May it not be that much of the
deep bitterness with which generations of Frenchmen
have viewed their national disaster has been due to

the same excess of self-assertion on our part of which the Prussians have complained ?

Since the publication of the First Edition, some valuable and wholly original details relating chiefly to the crowning event of the campaign—the Battle of Waterloo itself—have reached the Author, who has felt justified in adding them to this work, although thereby slightly enlarging its original scope.

Some of the numerous kind critics of this work have supposed that these Lectures had been actually delivered before publication. This was not so, however. They were not written until the Author had left the Staff College, although they embody the results of a study which was carried on there, as it had been begun years before he was connected with that Institution.

ALDERSHOT: 19*th April*, 1869.

PREFACE

THE FIRST EDITION.

————◦◦◦————

IT has been the practice at the Institution which the Author lately quitted, to commence the course of Military Art and History by the critical study of a single great campaign; that of Waterloo being, for obvious reasons, generally selected. In perusing much literature bearing on the subject, he has been constantly led to make two observations: the one, that critics of Napoleon and of the Allies are alike apt to build up theories upon inaccurate and superficial study of the facts; the other, that the key to the whole, the great strokes of strategy upon which the world's fate hung for a brief space, are apt to be lost, or greatly obscured, beneath a mass of pictorial details, interesting for the day to the families or friends of those who shared in the actions, but of little real importance to the general result. In addition to these tendencies, there is the third and more dangerous error of the so-called national historians, who wilfully pander to the passions of their countrymen at the expense of historical truth.

In laying before the world the result of his own study, the Author desires to claim no more credit for it than that he has striven for impartiality, and sought to apply to the narratives he has used the proper test of evidence. If, in doing this, it has been necessary to do battle specially with certain brilliant falsehoods, it is because these have their influence over millions of his fellow-men, and for that reason the more need to be thoroughly exposed.

He has endeavoured to confine his own criticisms, so far as is possible, to matters of actual evidence and fact. Where comments go beyond these he has sought rather to point to those of authors who have shown themselves practical soldiers as well as sound critics, than to offer observations which might reasonably be rejected as the mere dogmas of a Professor.

R.E. ESTABLISHMENT, CHATHAM :
October 24, 1868.

WATERLOO LECTURES.

——◆◇◆——

LECTURE I.

INTRODUCTION TO THE STUDY OF THE WATERLOO CAMPAIGN.

MILITARY HISTORY, if aspiring to be anything higher than the bare record of warlike transactions, must be accompanied by intelligent criticism. Of the limits of such criticism it is proposed to speak hereafter. At present our first duty is to consider what is the just and safe foundation on which both narrative and comment should rest; how, in short, we are to verify the facts on which we propose to build our theories. For, surely, without historic truth to light us through the past, it is vain to form judgments on it, or to seek to deduce lessons for the future.

To show by what principle such truth can alone be secured, I would here employ the words of a late writer, universally allowed to be one of the greatest critics which this age has produced. The lamented

B

Sir G. Cornewall Lewis, in a notable passage of his 'Credibility of the Early Roman History,' thus lays down the true law which should constantly guide our researches :—'It seems,' he says, 'to be often believed, and, at all events, it is perpetually assumed in practice, that historical evidence is different in its nature from other sorts of evidence. Until this error is effectually extirpated, all historical researches must lead to uncertain results. *Historical evidence, like judicial evidence, is founded on the testimony of credible witnesses.*'

It need hardly be pointed out that this law is quite as necessary in studying military events as any others. Indeed, there are none in which an actor is so apt to mistake mere impressions of his own for facts, and (which is very important) to note down for the use of history his own guesses at what exists and what occurs on the other side, instead of waiting to correct these from the proper source, the information which that other side alone can furnish of its means and objects. Unhappily, these hasty guesses are often more flattering than would be the truth to national vanity. Hence a powerful sentiment is enlisted on the side of error, and succeeding authors think they are doing their country service by shutting their eyes to the truth, and following blindly the narratives of their own party, thus accepting for history a purely onesided version of events. By and by the stereotyped statement is treated as fact, its accuracy hotly defended, records diligently searched in as far as they are likely to confirm it.   This process, continued on either side, multiplies contradiction, until essayists moralise over the falsity of history, forgetful that in all disputes truth can only be sifted out by comparing evidence, and that it is the special duty of the judge to correct that partiality of witnesses which obscures but does not change the nature of the facts.

We shall have in these pages to deal much with the military literature of a great neighbouring nation, whose writers sin above all others in the matter of their national defeats and victories.   It is not intended, however, to assume that our own are blameless.   The popular English version of that great battle which gives its name to the campaign of 1815 is hardly less a romance than the famous Waterloo chapter in Victor Hugo's 'Les Misérables,' over which our critics have with good reason made merry.   Let us select from our various school histories one of the best known, and see what is said of the Prussian share in the victory of Waterloo.   Of nearly a page devoted to the battle, just two short sentences are allotted to Blücher's part !   'When night approached, the heads of the Prussian columns were seen advancing to share in the combat.'   'The Prussians, who were comparatively fresh, continued the pursuit' [the French are described as broken entirely by Wellington's charge], 'and the army of Napoleon was virtually annihilated.'   What English lad, reading a story thus written, could possibly surmise that the fiercest

Pinnock's Gold-smith, 18th ed.

of all modern leaders of war was on the ground with part of his army at half-past four, was hotly engaged with Napoleon's reserves three hours before dark, had brought 50,000 fine troops into action at the time of Wellington's grand charge, and had 7,000 of them killed and wounded that evening in his vigorous support of our army! Yet these facts are perfectly patent to him who sees the battle of Waterloo, not as coloured by patriotic artists, but as portrayed by true history, and is willing to take his account of what the Prussians did, not from the guesses of enemy or ally, but direct from their own narratives, confirmed by those of independent observers.

It has been intimated that French historians offend terribly in this matter. They sin, not merely by omission, but by wilful repetition of error from book to book, long after the truth has been given to the world. This would matter little to us, comparatively, were French historians and French material for history not specially important to our own. Unhappily, the ease and grace of the military writers of France, and the number and accessibility of their works, have caused those of our country to adhere almost entirely to their versions of European wars, excepting always those in which English armies are mixed up. This slavish following of guides too often blind has warped our whole judgment of Continental military powers. We could hardly, indeed, have chosen worse for our teachers. No German writer would dream of sitting down deliberately to construct a

history of a war, a campaign, or even an action
between French and Germans, without carefully con-
sulting the French authorities as well as those of his
own nation.   A Frenchman, writing at this present
time of an affair of the revolutionary or imperial
period, thinks nothing of following implicitly the
bulletins of the day even for the enemy's numbers ;
or will take these at second-hand from some intermediate writer, with perfect good faith no doubt, but
with an utter disregard of the rules of evidence.   I
take as an instance the latest of such narratives, from
a work which, however little accurate, is yet one well
suited for its special purpose, being published as a
French Reader for the use of a great military college.
It is written by a Frenchman who seems able in his
method, perfectly honest-minded, and who, living in
this country permanently, is removed above all petty
reasons for flattering the national vanity of his own.
He is sketching the lives of some eminent French
generals, from whose writings he wishes to quote, and
among others that of Marshal Jourdan, with his great
achievement, the victory of Fleurus, which turned
the tide of the war in the Netherlands in 1794.
As the authorities employed are solely of the one
side, one knows beforehand how the estimate of
numbers will be given ; ' 100,000 Allied troops were
opposed to 70,000 Republicans.'   The author is but
following a host of writers who reckon no French but
those actually engaged, and who have never sought
to verify the original guess of their countrymen at

the strength of Coburg's beaten army. Yet the numbers of the latter have been published these twenty years from official returns in a standard Austrian work, and from this source the supposed 100,000 are found, by a single reference, to be just 45,775 ! As to the French, their available strength under Jourdan appears from Thiers' account (not likely to exaggerate in that direction) to have been full 81,000, when his reserves are reckoned. So the Republican general, instead of having only seven-tenths the force of his adversaries, commanded in reality not far from two to their one !

Düller's Erzherzog Karl, p. 211.

See Thi. Hist.Révo. vi. 395–398.

Whilst on the subject of French inaccuracies I may with advantage refer to a notable correspondence to be found in the appendix to the first volume of the life of that peerless military historian, the writer of the 'Peninsular War.' Here M. Thiers, the great master of the art of explaining away national mishaps, has fallen into the hands of an antagonist in every way his match, and is fairly worsted, even as to his French numbers, by the aid of the genuine returns, kept for Napoleon's private use, and still existing in the Paris archives. The discussion is a model of its kind on Napier's side ; and the airy readiness with which M. Thiers, unable to refute his adversary's facts, declines to argue further with 'interested or ignorant critics,' may serve to forewarn us how far the author of ' The Consulate and Empire ' can safely be trusted as an historical guide.

Life of Sir W. Napier, edited by Bruce, vol. i. App.

There are errors less important than those which

have been referred to, that become woven into ordinary histories from the mere careless habit of writers who, without intending to mislead, copy tamely the assertions of those who have gone before them, and take no pains to check their truth.   An amusing instance of such is to be found in the popular accounts of the great cavalry combat which closed the battle of Eckmuhl in 1809.   A French writer of mark, General Pelet (who served in the action, though he did not see the combat), ascribed the success of his countrymen to the superiority of the armour of the French Cuirassiers, who wore back as well as breastplates, over that of the Austrians of the same arm, who were protected only in front.   Pelet no doubt had some camp story for his authority for this strange assertion, which has been repeated again and again, and is recorded as an interesting fact by Alison, none of those who have borrowed the statement having enquired what help the French cavaliers really obtained in their successful charges from their armour behind, nor, what is more to the purpose, what was the actual proportion of the numbers of the combatants.   It so happens, however, that there are unusually complete records on both sides, from which the latter may be extracted.   Baron Stutterheim wrote a history for the Austrians, which, by favour exceptional at Vienna, was published at once, and forms a standard German authority.   Thiers, following Pelet, and using the French archives, has reckoned up the French cavalry with much elaboration.   An examination of these

Compare
Thi. x.119,
with Pro-
fessor
Schneida-
wind's,
1809, i. 51,
52. sources shows twelve squadrons of Austrian reserve
Cuirassiers, aided by seventeen of light cavalry (which
had suffered very severely just before), opposed to ten
full regiments of French heavy horse, aided by three
brigades of allied Germans. The latter had numbered
altogether 10,000 a few days before, the former little
over 3,000 : and, making the necessary allowance for
the preceding operations, this wonderful tale of a victory due to the armour on the backs of the victors
resolves itself into a hopeless stand of the Austrian
cavalry against a force more than three times their
strength.

It has not unfrequently occurred that the features
of national policy bear the impress of false current
notions of military events. Our own recent Indian
history affords a very striking instance of this truth.
Rather more than a quarter of a century since we
occupied Affghanistan, to anticipate Russian intrigue
on our north-western frontier. The country was
held for us by three separate brigades of troops, each
with distinct cantonments and administration. An
insurrection took place at the capital, spreading soon
to other districts ; and the force at head-quarters,
overcome rather by the imbecility of mismanagement
than by the strength of the enemy, perished absolutely with all its camp-followers in the attempt to
retreat. The other two brigades held their own
with perfect success, and maintained our hold of the
country until, being reinforced, they re-conquered it
with ease. We had thus lost about one-third of the

original army of occupation, 4,500 men in fact. Unfortunately, in writing of such a disaster, there is a tendency in the historian to magnify his office and give the event undue proportions, and the school of writers who seek effect rather than strict truth have made the Affghan war their own. Hence it has been usual to add to our actual losses the swarm of followers who attended the combatants that fell, and to keep in the background the true proportion of the latter to the forces that held out ; so that now-a-days, if twenty fairly informed Englishmen were interrogated on the subject, nineteen would probably unhesitatingly admit such statements as that ' all our army was destroyed,' or that ' our terrible loss of 16,000 men in Affghanistan shook our prestige throughout the East ; ' and the moral effect of the disaster upon our policy has been magnified threefold by misconception. It is not here sought to advocate any change in the pacific attitude adopted by our rulers on that frontier, but to show that it has been imposed by public opinion rooted on a misstatement of facts, and to gather from this instance the inference that a nation's policy may be largely influenced by the incorrect history of a war.

More remarkable than any such isolated mistake, and far more important in its bearings, is the persistent error of the French nation as to its own modern military annals. By excluding from sight Peninsular failures, by treating the Republican disasters of 1793 and 1795 as of no account in the light of alternate successes, by dwelling constantly on Napoleon's victories, and elaborating excuses for his defeats, their writers have striven to impregnate that great people with the dangerous belief that their land can produce at will soldiers invincible, and a chief that cannot err. Hence the ambitious policy which can be satisfied with nothing less than a sort of supremacy in Europe, such as Napoleon for the time actually secured. It would seem as though the feverish visions which lured that great genius to his ruin have infected more or less the whole nation that raised him to power. The belief that but for a series of unlucky accidents, but for treachery, but for some hostile element, Frenchmen under Napoleon could never have failed, has become almost a religious faith with decades of millions; and the natural consequence of this false view of history is the false policy which alarms and irritates the neighbouring peoples. This conviction of their military invincibility has been impressed by the French to some extent on others, so that among ourselves it used commonly to be taken for granted that, in the next collision between France and Germany, the armies of the latter would succumb. Those who study the history of modern wars more carefully, who discern how large a part of the French victories there recorded was due to the personal genius of one man, and observe how soon, when once made careless by success, that one in his turn met with ruinous defeat, do not so easily admit this assumption; least of all was it accepted among that great nation whose annals could match Jena with Rosbach, Dresden with Leipsic, Valmy with Waterloo, and who, if not so boastful, were scarcely less confident than their rivals. When Prussia armed against France, she might surely with as fair reason hope to revive the glories of Frederic as her rival those of Napoleon. And if a struggle, forced on by French arrogance, turned to the ruin of France, and of her chosen dynasty, that ruin was the direct result of the false teachings, which began with perverting history, and ended in the assertion of geographical claims impossible to admit, and pretensions which threatened the independence of her neighbours.

It has been said that intelligent criticism forms a vital part of sound military history. Let us here distinguish the two chief classes of critical remarks which writers employ; for their objects are essentially different.

In the first place, a campaign, or movement, or action, may be regarded as exemplifying some general theory. Correctness is, of course, as much an object here as in treating these subjects with any other view; but the conduct of individuals matters little, except in so far as it harmonises with or violates certain rules. The actors in this case are regarded simply as instruments, more or less imperfect, for carrying out certain designs, and are made subordinate in importance to the principles which it is the object to establish or to illustrate. This is that theoretical use of military history which has often met hot opposition, and which may easily become an abuse in the hands of those who mistake men for machines, and overlook the realities of war in their haste to reduce its combinations to geometrical rules. On the other hand, we have the distinct assurance of great commanders that professional study in some form is the first condition of practical success. Napoleon laid down this as an especial rule. The Archduke Charles practised it in his own person before taking a command-in-chief. Wellington, reticent to his own friends and lieutenants, was found ready, in

See Bruce's Life of Sir W. Napier, i. 147.

the midst of Peninsular triumphs, to discuss strategical questions with a young officer of his army when he could find one worthy of his confidence ; and on another occasion, at the close of his last great cam-

Kenn. p. 28.

paign, confessed to a junior staff-officer his personal obligation to daily study. The military, in fact, can never be an exception to that rule of other professions, which requires in their most brilliant ornaments something more than the rough practical knowledge which every useful member must possess. The day is gone by when great nations will look to see heaven-born generals appear at the first call to lead their armies. The very existence of such an institution among us as a Staff College, shows that in this country the higher branches of military art are receiving due attention. It is to avoid giving undue prominence to mere theory, to use the latter only in strict relation to known facts, that the course of study at the college is begun—as has been the practice since its opening—by a close historical survey of some great campaign, like that of Waterloo, the special subject of this work.

In making such a survey there is occasion to use another sort of criticism than that which merely dissects events to find the rules which govern them. This is that which deals with the characters and conduct of the men concerned. An event may be traced in all its leading features, its influence on the course of the campaign may be noted, but the task of the historian still remains unfulfilled if he fail to assign, in some degree at least, the relation to the whole of the chief actors and their parts. This particular campaign affords abundant scope for pains in this respect. No other in its result so deeply affects national vanity. No other is regarded from so many points of view. No other has exercised so much ingenuity and industry on the part of writers striving to obscure or to bring out the truth. In this its strictly historical aspect, it is as specially suited to the critic as to the student of strategy for the value of its lessons. Compact in time, important in result, conducted by the chief generals of the world, at the very prime of their reputation, and being, as it were, the finished result of the experience of twenty years' war, we may here, if anywhere, look to see skill, conduct, and forethought taking the place of blind chance, and to find the operations leading up, step by step, to a perfect end. And just such an end was the battle of Waterloo, which, by the greatness of its issue and its peculiarly national character, has not only thrown other equally important actions into the shade, but has actually imposed itself, falsely as it were, on the world as the special object of attention in this campaign. Yet not on this battle—as I hope presently to show—however heroically fought or dexterously won, should the glory of the Allied generals rest; but on the noble devotion of each to the common object in view, and the perfection of mutual confidence which enabled each so to act separately as to produce with their united armies at the right moment the greatest possible result. Never in the whole of military history was the tactical value of the troops more entirely subordinated to the strategical operations. He knows not what the battle of Waterloo was who views in it merely the shock of two great armies, English and French, continued through a fierce day's fighting, until the superior endurance of the British line shatters and finally overthrows their exhausted enemy. The eye that sees this in it and sees no more, forgetful of the long columns toiling through deep muddy lanes on the French flank, the sturdy legions of North Germans with clenched teeth and straining limbs forcing their guns through mire and over obstructions, the fierce old chieftain who is seen wherever his encouragement is needed, and everywhere is greeted as their ' father ' by those he urges on, the cool and disciplined staff who are preparing to make the most decisive use of the coming masses in the assault on their hated enemy, does not only monstrous injustice to Blücher and his army, but robs Wellington of his due. For Wellington regarded not the matter thus. He knew and looked for the approaching army of his ally as part of the fight; he watched from early afternoon the lessening pressure which told that Napoleon was forced to draw away his reserves from the main battle; above all, he had prepared, in concert with the old Prince-Marshal, this fatal stroke of war; and not to understand or to ignore this, is to miss the real design with which the fight was joined. Waterloo was, in fact, viewed in its proper aspect, but the crown and finish of a splendid piece of strategy. It is into the details of this that we now propose to look, with the aid of the best writers on the subject.

Of these let us first speak of the Prussian. Most important among them is Baron Müffling, Military Commissioner with Wellington's army. Forming the confidential link between the staffs of the Allied Marshals, living with the one, and fully conversant with all the feelings of the other, his general knowledge of their side of the campaign must have been equal, at the least, to that of any other man. As Quarter-master-General to Blücher in the preceding years, he had seen much of war on the grandest scale, and was especially observant of the system of Napoleon, of which he knew the weak points at that time more thoroughly, judging from the notes he has left us, than any other of the Allied chiefs. His opinion on military matters carries the weight which all men will allow to that of one who has mastered his craft thoroughly in all points of view. A student of theory in youth, he had attained on the field staff a high position by his merits, and had trained his mind by methodical practice to judge of the largest tactical movements, as a drill-sergeant does of the evolutions

Mü. Mem. p. 129.

of his squad. A man who could time exactly the march of the enemy's cavalry round the flank of a retiring force, or of the infantry of a whole wing of

Ibid. pp. 60, 61.

their army seeking to gain and deploy in a given position, was just the balance needed to regulate the movements of Blücher, or rather of the clear-sighted but impulsive and chivalric Gneisenau, whose advice the old Marshal followed. Complete in theory, sound and careful in practice, very disagreeable possibly to know, as he certainly was dogmatic and censorious in his professional view of others, Müffling presents to us the highest type of a carefully elaborated staff-officer of the old Prussian model. His personal employment near Wellington makes him a most valuable evidence, his private jealousy of Gneisenau a tolerably impartial one, as to the share of the great Englishman in the common achievement of the Allied armies. He has left us a short history of the campaign, published in January, 1816, and translated soon after ; also a more valuable account in his memoirs, known in its English dress as ' Passages out of my Life.' To both of these we shall have frequent occasion to refer.

There is a well-known Prussian official account of the events of 1815, compiled for the Berlin Government by a Major Wagner, and often quoted under his name. It is cold and dry as a narrative, but elaborately complete ; and forms, of course, the best groundwork for the inner details of the Prussian army. For their orders, movements, and numbers we shall look chiefly here.

There is another complete Prussian account by Von Damitz, an officer who served through the campaign in a high post. But as this work shows neither the laboured correctness of the official one, nor the original information of Müffling's, nor the genius which gilds the most technical disquisitions in that of Clausewitz, it has not been found necessary to make such detailed use of it as might multiply references needlessly without throwing further light upon the subject. For the same reason the excellent narrative to be found in the 14th volume of the standard German 'History of the Revolutionary Wars,' by Schulz, will not be cited here, though it would repay the special student for his perusal ; as would still more that in the 'History of Russia,' by Bernhardi, whose researches—unknown to the writer when this work was first published—will be found strongly to confirm certain criticisms ventured on, especially as regards the all-important day after Ligny.

Varnhagen von Ense's 'Life of Blücher' is valuable for its anecdotical details ; but is of too popular and sketchy a character to be of much value to the military critic.

Clausewitz's 'Campaign of 1815' deserves particular

attention, as well for his personal knowledge of the events, as for two other special reasons. In the first place, Wellington himself deemed this general's criticisms of sufficient importance to require an elaborate answer from his own pen, a compliment he paid no other of his censors. In the second, Clausewitz in his own country stands confessedly at the head of all military theorists ; and the great reputation made for him by the genius his writings display, deepens constantly with time. It is a matter of public acknowledgment that the principles which he bequeathed to his countrymen in his great work ' On War,' for the guidance of their action in their next struggle, were acted on fully in the recent contests which have placed Prussia at the head of Germany, and caused her to appear the first military power of the world.

Published in the Sup. Disp. vol. x. and in Gleig's 'Brialmont,' ii. App.

Belgian writers should not be wholly neglected in treating of a campaign fought in their country, although it must be observed that Colonel Charras has ransacked the local sources of information with exhaustive effect. Brialmont is the most important for our purpose, and his ' History of Wellington ' has, under Mr. Gleig's fostering care, become a household work in our land. It is a strange instance of the fascination which Napoleon's genius exercises over even powerful minds, that Brialmont, like our own Napier, appears partially blinded by it, and has in consequence done himself and his subject less than justice in that short portion of his second volume which treats of the Waterloo Campaign. His details are

here less perfect, his treatment less clear, his judgments less lucid by far than in his Peninsular chapters. He seems to have assumed beforehand, like a
hundred other less praiseworthy writers, that Napoleon could never greatly err in strategical difficulties,
and to have determined that the blame of his defeat
must lie on other shoulders. Hence in one strange Brial. ii. p. 281.
passage on a particular disputed event, he appears to
rest censure for a certain delay upon Marshal Ney in
the text, though, in a note to the page, the error is
clearly charged to the Emperor instead, as though
the author could not bring himself to write in large
print, ' here Napoleon failed.'

The plain account of the Dutch writer, Van Loben
Sels, is far more complete as a history, contains many
original documents, and is an essential authority as
regards the details which concern the troops of the
Netherlands that fought under Wellington.

The literature of Austria (deeply concerned as she
was in the great issue) contributes nothing towards
our knowledge of the campaign of 1815, if we except
the valuable report made to his imperial master by
Baron Vincent, Military Commissioner for the Court
of Vienna with Wellington. This paper is to be found See p. 24.
in the British work called ' Official Documents,' and
will be referred to in its proper place. The silence of
the Austrian military writers is the less extraordinary
when it is remembered that they have left the tale of
their own country's victory of Neerwinden, which
cleared Belgium of French invaders in 1793 as

effectually as that of Waterloo twenty-two years later,
to be known in European history almost solely through
the loose and contradictory versions of the defeated
Republican generals.　No Austrian detailed account
of this remarkable triumph (which cost the van-
quished 4,000 men left upon the field, 10,000 fugitives
lost in the retreat, and the possession of Belgium) ever
appeared until 1808, and then only in an obscure professional journal.　Almost all known histories of it
accept as authentic, and use freely the hasty dispatch
of the beaten general Dumourier, written to excuse
his disaster, which is flatly contradicted by that of
Miranda, who personally commanded the wing that
was driven off the field, and proves by its wording
that the former was unacquainted with the part played
by that wing, the ground it occupied, or the correct
names of the villages it attacked.　Indeed, in attempting to use both accounts, the anonymous writer of
the ' Victories ' has naturally found it impossible to
make them harmonise, and to escape the difficulty he
quotes Miranda indeed, but with audacity excelling
that of other French historians excusing national
defeats, quotes him with the hours mentioned in his
original letter altered to suit those given by Dumourier
and with no notice of the alteration !　This shameless
falsification of the less popular version becomes immediately apparent on a comparison of the quotation
with the original ' Correspondence de Miranda,' from
which it professes to be taken.　But Dumourier's inventions would never have been embodied into history,

had Austria not left the field of military literature open for her enemies to work their will in.

We now pass to English authors. Of these the earliest that deserves attention is Siborne, whose work, with its excellent atlas, has the honour of being the first thoroughly complete narrative of the campaign ever issued. Even now it forms a most useful book of reference; nor can any student peruse it without being under obligation to the writer for the diligence with which he has collected his materials, and the care with which he has used them. At the same time it must be confessed that it has the essential faults of a national history written soon after a great war. Much that is in it would never have been inserted had the work not been largely dependent for support at its publication on the British army. As to the view taken of the Great Duke, it is simply that taken of Napoleon by a Napoleonist writer; the view in fact of an advocate who believes that his hero was incapable of mistakes, and cannot suffer him to be charged with any. The book is thoroughly British, no doubt, but hardly suited for general use; nor is this surprising when we recollect the time at which it appeared. The weakness of all such national versions is that they can hardly hope for acceptance save among the nation whose taste they are intended to meet.

Sir Archibald Alison's great work has of course a large section on our subject. We shall not, however, refer to it, for though very readable, as are all accounts of campaigns by that distinguished author, it will not help our present purpose. It is true that the errors which disfigured this part of the earlier editions, disappeared to a great extent in that of 1860, for which the campaign appears to have been nearly re-written, to the great improvement of the work as a whole. In his later years Alison had taken more pains to attain the accuracy he formerly neglected. By the aid of such sound authorities as Charras and Clause-witz, the English historian at length produced a Water-loo narrative not only interesting, but useful in detail. In seeking for the picturesque, however, he has lessened the value of his chapters, by devoting the larger part of their space to those battle-scenes into which he loved to throw his strength, to the neglect of the story as a whole. However popular these episodes of combat may be, their description, espe-tially by writers who have not seen war, can little help the practical student. It is right to add that Alison has, in this his latest study on the subject, used very freely, and with due acknowledgment, the brief but pregnant criticisms on the campaign, of Colonel Hamley in his essay on ' Wellington's Career.' Such light as he has thrown on the strategy he appears to owe mainly to the Waterloo pages of that brilliant sketch.

In one English authority we have the evidence of a sound eye-witness happily combined with the gift of clear expression, and the faculty of judicial criti-cism, which make history valuable: for all these qualities appear plainly in the posthumous work of the late Sir J. Shaw Kennedy, a most valuable addition to the literature of the campaign. The writer was employed on the staff of Wellington, received orders personally from him in the crisis of the battle of Waterloo, and has left in his pages such a clear record of its chief phases, and of the marvellous tact and readiness of his great chief, as can nowhere else be found. Though his volume is mostly devoted to the battle itself, he has taken occasion to review the strategy which preceded it, with a freedom and breadth that no English author before him had used. The reflections of such a tried soldier and honest critic upon the commander whom he revered have special weight. His admiration of Wellington's tactical skill—a skill to which perhaps full justice had never before been rendered—has not led him into the common mistake of supposing his hero a demigod beyond all error or criticism. The principle upon which he boldly examines the strategy on either side may best be given in his own words, which may be quoted as specially deserving attention for their bearing on our subject. 'There is an error almost universal as regards the bulk of mankind, in supposing that great commanders, such as Napoleon, Wellington, Cæsar, and Hannibal, did not commit great mistakes. The game of war is so exciting, so complicated, and presents so many propositions which are capable of a variety of solutions, and which must be solved irrevocably on the instant, that no human

Kenn. p. 150.

powers of mind can reach further than a comparative excellence as a great commander ; that is, great commanders will have higher views, act upon superior principles, and commit fewer errors than ordinary men ; but still this is only comparative merit, and should not exempt the operations of even the greatest commanders from criticism.'

Ante, p.18. Wellington's own Memorandum, already referred to, forms most valuable material for history, as do the Dispatches of that great general. But such papers as these (like the mass of letters, bulletins, and reports in the volume of ' Official Documents ' published in London soon after the campaign), being written ostensibly from a single point of view, and limited to a certain definite purpose, do not, taken by themselves, serve as histories of the whole event in which their authors took part.

Hooper's ' Waterloo ' is one of the best single volumes on this campaign existing in any language : indeed, were we reduced to one book in studying it, this would be perhaps the one to adhere to. Mr. Hooper, like the French critic Quinet, has followed Charras very closely, and is under very large obligations (not wholly unacknowledged) to the latter writer for his historical details and his criticisms of Napoleon. On the whole his work may be declared more complete than his French rival Quinet's, and more compact and readable than that of the great historian to whose researches both are so much indebted. His able defence of Wellington's conduct, when impugned at certain points, is always worthy attention : yet it is rather that of an advocate than a judge ; and in this respect his work falls in value far behind that of Sir J. Kennedy. On the other hand, no English student of the whole campaign can afford to neglect the narrative of Hooper, unless indeed he has time to master those more original authorities, which the author has skilfully condensed into a moderate octavo volume.

Two classes of writers, of views diametrically opposed, claim our interest when we pass to those of France. The one comprehends the long list of worshippers who so adore the military genius of Napoleon, as to be unable to discern the flaws in their idol. So complete, in their eyes, was his conception, and so perfect his execution of all warlike operations, that failure must be held impossible, as far as his own conduct could affect the result. In all his misfortunes, and in that of Waterloo above all, some other reason must be found for the want of his usual success ; and as national vanity forbids the disaster being laid on the quality of French troops, ingenuity is racked for third causes, which shall spare the honour of the Emperor and his legions. Let his own political errors, the treachery or imbecility of his subordinates, special conditions of weather, blundering good luck on his opponent's side, be charged with his ruinous defeat. If none of these will serve the purpose, ' an unhappy fatality ' must be found at every turn, such as makes brave men over-prudent, brilliant men slow,

old soldiers rash at the wrong moments; so that an
unheard-of combination of others' mistakes was the
true cause of the ruin of Napoleon. Let all or any
such excuses be employed rather than believe that he
was ever wanting to his army, or his army to its chief.
Of such authors as these, who suit their facts to their
ideas, and use historical material only so far as it
serves to embellish their idol, a library might be
formed, and formed to little advantage. We shall
take but one into our list—one who has surpassed the
rest no less in his worship of Napoleon's military
genius, than in the success of the great work in which
he has striven to perpetuate error. Of this, the well-
known 'Consulate and Empire,' we shall say a few
words later, as well as of Napoleon's own writings
on the subject.

France has no longer any necessity to give herself
up to this phantom of history. Writing in her own
tongue, and born of her own race, there has of late
arisen a severe school of critics who absolutely refuse
to follow their predecessors in blind adulation of
Napoleon, whether viewed as soldier or Emperor.
These have gone to work upon the Waterloo campaign
with the cool deliberation of anatomists, dissecting
the limbs of the dead to find the true causes of the
malady. Facts are what they first seek, and conclu-
sions drawn only from facts are to follow. They
pursue, indeed, the true historical method; and, as
their national pride is enlisted on the side of France,
there is no fear of any general injustice being wrought

to the French cause under their treatment. Conspicuous among such authors are Charras and Quinet, and, for the reason just given, their works are invaluable to us as independent students of this campaign. General Jomini might also have been added to this list of sound critics, but that the peculiar form of his narrative (supposed to flow from the Emperor himself) fatally hampers him in matters of which Napoleon has actually written, and written much that history refuses to accept as true. This makes his work far less valuable as to 1815 than in those portions which relate to campaigns of which Napoleon has forborne to speak personally. There is, however, an independence in the spirit of this writer which forbids his yielding his judgment to Napoleon's in matters of opinion ; and his criticisms on the campaign have, therefore, the proper value of those falling from one whose great practical knowledge of war is only exceeded by his devotion to theory.

To return to the modern school of French critics. Colonel Charras is, and will probably continue to be, the first of all authorities on the Waterloo Campaign. As a soldier he had seen hot service in Algeria ; and afterwards holding office in the Bureau of War under the brief republic of 1848, he had all the technical knowledge which could aid in throwing light upon the subject. Being banished from France in 1851, he took up his abode in Belgium, and revenged his cause with the most severe yet honourable weapon that exile ever took in hand. Whilst living on the scene of Napoleon's last campaign, he undertook to write for his fellow-countrymen a true history of that great disaster; and if he has not shaken the throne of the Third Napoleon, he has at least struck rude blows at the idolatry with which the name of the First was regarded. Doubtless his own political career must have sent him to his work with much bitterness at heart against the dynasty to whom he owed his banishment; but though his leanings are against the defeated Emperor, he has striven from first to last to judge of nothing without sufficient original proof. His work is truly exhaustive. 'After its perusal,' as he fairly says in the preface, 'one man will seem somewhat lowered; but, on the other hand, the French army will appear greater, and France less humbled.' No part of this great book is uninteresting, and the care which he has bestowed on it extends even to the Atlas which accompanies it for the student's use. It must be remarked, however, that the very pains with which Colonel Charras traces out his details, and gives, in the body of his text or in notes, a multiplicity of original documents, detracts from the natural liveliness of his style, and makes the work almost too bulky and diffuse for common use. This is especially noticeable in the more recent editions, which, except in a single necessary instance (p. 101), will not be referred to, the earlier one of 1858 being used elsewhere throughout.

That of M. Quinet in this respect far surpasses it.

This writer originally intended solely to review the
book of Colonel Charras, and make known to his
countrymen its incomparable worth. In performing
this self-imposed task he found occasion to refer to
many original documents not specially used before,
and being also a resident in Belgium, he took pains,
like the author he was following, to personally examine the theatre of war. Gifted with clearness of
vision to find the truth, and with a trenchant style
well suited for sharp exposure of falsehood, he has
skilfully followed up the path first opened by Charras.
Certain stories, long accepted by French writers, have
been so effectually handled by this keen critic, that
for all readers open to conviction by evidence, they
must disappear from the domain of history. His
work, though hardly attaining the dignity of a history,
may be called, as regards both style and matter, the
most brilliant review of the campaign ever written.
Before his sharp strokes vanish, their magic power
dispelled by the touch of truth, those mythic notions
of this great struggle, which have too long stood in
place of facts, and which he has happily named ‘La Quin. p. 7.
Légende Napoléonienne.’

The real author of these fables, in their first origin,
was Napoleon himself. Not content with supplying
the usual materials which all commanders of great
armies bequeath to history in their correspondence,
he has written two separate narratives of the campaign. The first of these appeared in the earliest
part of his St. Helena exile under the name of his

attendant, General Gourgaud ; but from the moment of its publication has been ascribed, without denial, to its true author. It is a nervous, forcible narrative, thrown hastily off, to enable the imperial writer to show to the world that he was not to blame for the disaster which had so humiliated France. No one more plainly than M. Thiers admits it to be superior in value and truthfulness to the more elaborate and studied apology to be found in the ' Mémoires.' To both of these it will be repeatedly necessary to refer. It is the former which, above all other misrepresentations, has misled the mass of historians. We do not propose to follow blindly those writers who have accepted it without applying to its details the ordinary rules of evidence. How hard it is to correct an error which has once crept into history, is well shown by the fact that although the ninth volume of the ' Mémoires ' (as finally published) contains its own refutation in the appended narrative of Colonel Heymès, and although in 1840 Marshal Ney's son published a mass of documents issued by Napoleon's staff in 1815, flatly contradicting in many points the versions of the Emperor, the latter have continued to be accepted as authentic by innumerable writers, and none even took the trouble to attempt to explain the discrepancies until M. Thiers applied himself to the task.

No one can peruse the twentieth volume of that great author's ' Consulate and Empire ' without doing homage to the powers which he has brought to his

Thi. p. 48, note.

task. If a brilliant style, large acquaintance with
details, special opportunities of correcting error, and a
full knowledge of the strength of the evidence against
his hero, would enable anyone at this time to clear
Napoleon of the responsibility of this great defeat,
M. Thiers might have succeeded. Had so clear-
sighted a writer entered on the subject with an
unbiassed mind, no one can doubt that he would
himself have seen where Napoleon failed. This was
not the case, however. He has undertaken beforehand to prove to all the world that Napoleon, culpable
as a man, mistaken as a ruler, was, as a captain, without stain or error. With many fine words about
truth, conscience, and the dignity of history, we find
mingled in the very first of his important notes on
the campaign the following sentence, in which his
real prejudice escapes him. ' We have here, in truth, Thi. xx.
to suppose several impossibilities in order to prove the 52, *note.*
incapacity at this juncture of one of the greatest of
known generals.' These *impossibilities* are merely to
believe that Napoleon did not give a certain order the
receipt of which has never been proved, which was not
carried out, and which is in contradiction with his own
later-written instructions, *but which ought to have been
given*, as it now appears. ' Call anything impossible '
(it is meant), ' rather than believe that the Emperor
mistook his strategy.' The author has written
throughout with the same foregone conclusion, and,
let us add it plainly, with a mischievous effect corresponding to the consummate power of his pen. No

other account of the campaign has been, perhaps ever
will be, so widely read, as the famous first chapter of
the twentieth volume.   It not only forms part of all
standard libraries, but, republished separately under
the simple name of ' Waterloo,' its yellow cover is
seen on every bookstall in France, and its pages have
become part of her household literature.   Since, therefore, no other historian on this side has written so
lately, so powerfully, or with such full information as
M. Thiers, we need take no other representative of the
military infallibility of Napoleon into our review.   In
his narrative are met the most charming language
and the worst faults of a host of authors whose works
are, for the most part, written but to pass away.
The presence of a Napoleon on the throne, the approval of the Academy, the lucid eloquence of its
style, have stamped this volume as the masterpiece
of that false school of history with which we are
so much concerned.   We shall have constant occasion to refer to it, and would here only say that,
in many passages defending Napoleon, M. Thiers
clearly has Charras in view, though not expressly
naming his antagonist.   If it were possible to rebut
the charges made by the latter against the Emperor,
it would, we may be sure, be here effectually done.
The skill with which the great national writer uses
every point of evidence which bears in favour of his
view, and hides from sight such as conflict with it,
proves him the most valuable of advocates whilst the
most dangerous of historians.   It is only the mighty

power of that truth which he professes to invoke, that enables a critic to dare to question his results. But he himself has said of the controversy, ' Truth is holy, and no just cause can suffer from it.' Seeking only for this truth, we proceed to the examination of the subject.

LECTURE II.

PREPARATIONS FOR THE CAMPAIGN.

' ON his return from Elba to the throne of France, Napoleon found the total of the land forces reduced by Louis XVIII. to 150,000, of which but 80,000 were available for a campaign. Judging 800,000 to be necessary for the defence of his recovered empire, he proceeded to raise three additional battalions to each regiment of the line, take all the sailors for shore duty, call out the National Guard, summon the pensioners to service, and refill the arsenals. In ten weeks France became one camp, with 560,000 men upon the rolls.' In some such words as these run the older accounts of the events of the Hundred Days, based Mém. viii. universally on a statement of Napoleon's own ; but 272. an examination of the records of the War Bureau of Paris has reduced the proportions of this achievement until it seems but little for so great an organiser. Cha. p. 41. From their evidence Charras has clearly shown that the real additions made to the army bequeathed by the fugitive Bourbon were just 53,000 to the total, and 43,000 to the real effective numbers, which stood on the 1st June at 198,000. From the dates of many of the orders given during his brief rule, and especially

those (of 1st May) as to the fortifying of Paris, it is Cha. p. 41.
almost certain that, on first reaching the Tuileries,
Napoleon did not realise to the full the immensity of
his danger in the fact of the determined hostility of
the Allied Sovereigns. If we compare with Charras'
exposition of the truth the statements of M. Thiers, as Thi. xx. 6.
favourable to the Emperor's own story as can be those
of anyone who has had access to the official records,
we find that the total embodied is given indeed by
the latter at 288,000 ; but that deductions of ineffec-
tives (for in the strain which the Empire was under, we
must assume that 66,000 given as at the depots were
men not really serviceable) reduce this to 196,000, a
number actually below that of Charras, though mar-
vellously near his as coming from a writer of such
different sympathies. It must be observed that these
two authors have worked at this point, and certain
others, from the same original authorities, but with
contrary views and objects. Here (as in similar
passages where they agree) we may safely follow
them, and assume it to be beyond all doubt that
Napoleon's effective field forces at the beginning of
June were rather less than 200,000 men. Against
him the coalition was rolling up on all the borders
of France such gigantic hosts as had never in all
history been moved together for a single object. Düller's
The Archduke Charles left the retreat to which, Erzherzog
Karl,
in disgust at a brother's perfidy, he had withdrawn p. 672.
six years before, and gathered a mixed army of
Austro-Germans on the Rhine. Schwartzenberg led

other Austrians to the same frontier.   More Austrians,
set free by the death of Murat, prepared to force the
Memoir
of Sir S.
Whitting-
ham, p.
278.
Alps and carry the war on from Italy.   Ferdinand
recalled English officers to lead over the Pyrenees the
Spanish troops which they had disciplined into success.   More formidable still in the distance, Russia
gathered legions estimated at a quarter of a million
to support the Austrians on the Rhine.   La Vendée,
faithful to her royalist traditions, rose against the
usurper.   Nearest and most dangerous of all, close
on the northern frontier of France, and within a few
days' march of her capital, the English general whose
name Napoleon's Spanish armies knew too well, and
the daring Prussian who had but lately ridden trium-
phantly into Paris, each at the head of a large army,
lay waiting for the signal to advance and crush the
man who defied the world in arms.   To this man,
whose life had been the history of Europe for the
previous fifteen years, upon whom all eyes were now
fixed as the sole author of the struggle, must we look
if we would see the central figure which gives the
drama of Waterloo its interest.   Rate Napoleon's
genius for politics or war as you will, the fact still is
there, that, by the circumstances of the time and the
nature of military events, his possible success or his
certain failure must be the chief matters of interest
in the story, the causes which led to his defeat the first
questions of importance for the student of any nation
to solve.

In the ' Mémoires ' Napoleon has given us at length

his motives for choosing the offensive, and we may Mem. viii. 285. believe that he has fairly stated them, since they agree with those published in his first history, and are such Gourg. p. 24. that he could have had no interest in their invention. It is here as well to state once for all, that where Napoleon, the author, does not contradict himself, is not contradicted by any other testimony, and has obviously no reason for distorting the facts, his evidence as to his own campaign is of the highest value : but that the 'Mémoires' should have been recklessly taken, even by English writers, for history, without weighing their statements by the common sense rules of evidence, is plain proof that this extraordinary man's genius has imposed on our countrymen very much as on the rest of the world.

To beat the Allies out of Belgium at a stroke before the Austrians were ready for action ; to gain that country to his side, with the Rhine barrier so dear to French soldier and politician ; the prospect (visionary enough, but Napoleon was essentially a man of visionary notions) of a change of Ministry in England, and of a movement in his favour among the small German States upon his first success ; such are his avowed motives for the invasion he attempted. On the other hand, as both his narratives admit, he was well aware that, if defeated, the defence of France would be a harder matter than ever : but the hope of dissolving the coalition by a master-stroke of victory, of destroy- Gourg. p. 26. ing separately the army of detested England, of carrying the war beyond those provinces of France which

had so lately felt its miseries, prevailed.   He resolved
Gourg.
p. 97.
to fall upon his enemies by the 15th June. ' Events,'
he writes afterwards, ' made his calculations fail ; but
the plan chosen was so conformable to military rules
that, despite its non-success, every man of sense will
agree that, in the like situation, it is that which should
be followed.'   If this be so, and yet the failure were
so complete, what does it prove but that his condition
was desperate, and his attempt to restore his throne
by arms the greatest of conceivable blunders ; or that
a perfect conception was most imperfectly executed ?

Into the plans of the Allied generals we need not
inquire, except so far as they bear upon what happened.   They had made certain arrangements (which
we shall presently examine) intended to meet the
event which occurred ; and now lay in their chosen
cantonments awaiting either Napoleon's attack, or the
coming up of the main body of those great masses of
which they formed but one wing.   The country
See Map.
which they had to guard, open by nature to invasion
in its western part along the whole frontier, from the
Meuse to the Straits of Dover, was yet much covered
by art.   Most of this district, lying west of a line
drawn north and south through Brussels, was in
charge of the English general, and his diligence had
already blocked many of its principal roads by repair-
ing the fortresses which commanded them.   The Prussians guarded the eastern half of the Netherlands,
Müff. Hist.
p. 70.
their troops (as one of their best authors admits)
placed more for convenience of supply than for concentration in haste.   One fortress alone, Namur, at the

junction of the Sambre and Meuse, was in their hands ;
but between them and France rose the steep bare
cold plateaux of the Ardennes, a country so difficult
to cross, and so utterly unproductive of food, that to
troops fed on Napoleon's system of living almost from
hand to mouth, it might be deemed impassable.   To
make this the line of attack was probably never con-
templated by Napoleon.   Certainly the Allied generals
did not expect him that way.   To attack by their
right near the sea, or by the central line which promised both to divide their armies and lead straight
to Brussels, were the contingencies admitted if he
attacked at all.   In either case he must face the
probability of being crushed by their larger forces,
as they very well knew.

Of his 198,000 actually available soldiers Napoleon
only found himself able to collect on the Belgian frontier, after making the most moderate detachments to
other quarters, an army which he himself calls 115,000, Gourg.
p. 31.
but which Charras with painful care proves to have Cha. p. 58.
numbered 128,000, inclusive of a train of 3,500 non-
combatants.   As Thiers admits 124,000 men present Thi. xx.21.
at the concentration, and excludes the train, there is no
substantial disagreement between these two authorities ; and we may safely say that Napoleon estimates
his own force 10,000 below the truth, forgetting
apparently that he thereby enhances the rashness of
his enterprise.   Holding fortresses occupied by depots
and National Guards on all the main roads leading
from the north-eastern and eastern frontier of France,
he might hope to collect his striking power at a single

point undiscovered.　The general situation and the strength of the Allied forces were known to him by secret intelligence.　On the other hand, they had information of his force which was at least equally good.

Gur. xii.
372.

As early as the 11th May, Wellington wrote to Sir H. Hardinge, his agent with Blücher, that he reckoned Bonaparte's means for attack at 110,000 men ; and somewhat later the Prussians had made a very exact

Sib. i.
App. X.

estimate of their enemy's field army, corps by corps, rating the whole at 130,000 men.　This knowledge

See p. 122.

curiously affected their reports of facts in the campaign, as will be hereafter observed.

We have said that Napoleon knew the general strength of the Allies.　Concerning this there have never been any of those great delusions which the French have indulged in with regard to the numbers of their enemies in former contests.　The authorities have been too many and too keen to allow of such illusions, and, what is still more to the purpose, the real disproportion was so great as to suffice for the national vanity of even their vainest writers.

Gourg.
p. 32.

The Prussian army, estimated by Napoleon himself at 120,000, was actually but little less.　It was divided into four grand corps, each complete in all the

Pr. Off.
p. 4.

arms.　These numbered in actual total within one hundred of the 117,000 combatants at which they are usually reckoned, and were thus distributed :—

1st Corps	(Zieten), about Charleroi .	31,000	nearly.
2nd ,,	(Pirch), about Namur .	32,000	,,
3rd ,,	(Thielemann), about Ciney	24,000	,,
4th ,,	(Bülow), about Liège . .	30,000	,,

It is right to add that Charras shows that the park Cha. App. Note C. of the army is excluded from these numbers, and that the proportion of artillerymen allotted to the guns in each corps is so small, that he has taken upon himself to increase it slightly.

The positions of the 1st and 2nd Corps along the See Map. Sambre enabled their outposts of cavalry to watch the line of frontier from Bonne Espérance, their western-most point, to the Meuse. Thielemann continued the chain along the edge of the Ardennes about Dinant, his headquarters having been advanced into the forest to enable him to guard the portion of it near that town, which is exceptionally open and easy to traverse. Bonne Espérance, from which the line was taken up by Wellington's army, lies only eight miles from Lobbes, where the Prussian posts crossed the Sambre, so that that river, on its passage from the French town of Maubeuge into Belgium, very nearly divided the sections of open frontier guarded by the Allies.

The numbers of Wellington's army are less easy to agree upon than those of the others. Estimated by Napoleon at 102,000, they have been reduced by Gourg. p. 33, n. Cha. p. 65. Charras to 95,000, from a very minute examination of all the records left of the campaign in Belgium. Siborne, however, brings the total up to 106,000, and Sib. i. 426. we must look a little closely to see the cause of so considerable a discrepancy. Examining the tables given by these two careful writers we find, as might be expected in this particular matter, that the

Englishman is the more correct. Charras says that he omits the Hanoverian *second brigade*, which was at Antwerp, and remained there during the campaign. Now, in the five Hanoverian brigades with Wellington in the early part of the spring, and in the campaign afterwards, there is no brigade numbered *second*, as all tables prove. But a corps of Hanoverians, 9,000 strong (called 10,000 in April), arrived with the chief Hanoverian general, Decker, later than the rest, and being formed into *four reserve brigades* was— after much difficulty as to its provisioning—left in garrison by Wellington. It is clear then how the difference arose, and how Charras was led into his error. As it was Wellington's own choice that these Hanoverians and certain other troops (amounting by Siborne's tables to 3,200 more) should not be taken into the field, there seems no good reason why they should be deducted from his strength.

Supp.
Disp. x.
383.

Sib. i. 32
and App.

This 106,000 was thus divided, for Wellington had now so far adopted the Continental model as to break the 70,000 bayonets of his field force into three great corps, keeping the cavalry separate in a fourth :—

1st Corps, Prince of Orange	25,000
2nd Corps, Lord Hill	24,000
Reserve Corps, under Wellington's personal orders .	21,000
Cavalry Corps, Lord Uxbridge	14,000
Artillery and Engineers (distributed among the Corps)	10,000
	94,000
Garrisons (sometimes reckoned in the Reserve Corps)	12,000
	106,000

The proper arrangement of the corps was (as Wel- Supp. Disp. x. 517. lington in his Reply to Clausewitz has specially noted) one of his hardest tasks. His fighting force of infantry was composed of six divisions of British troops, partly recruits, partly veterans, mixed with King's Germans of the Peninsular army, equal to any infantry in the world ; of five brigades of Hanoverian raw troops ; of three and a half divisions of Dutch-Belgians ; of a Brunswick division ; and of a Nassau brigade. Each of these had their own officers' staff and regimental organisation, which must be left untouched. Accordingly the Hanoverian brigades were distributed through each of his five British divisions of infantry of the line, the 1st or Guards division being alone of English troops. Then the whole were arranged in corps. The 1st and 3rd English divisions, and Chassé and Perponcher with their divisions of Dutch-Belgians, formed the 1st Corps. The 2nd and 4th divisions, and the rest of the Dutch-Belgians, made up the 2nd Corps. The Reserve included the 5th and 6th divisions, the Brunswickers, and the Nassauers. The cavalry were combined nominally into one command, but were, as in all Wellington's campaigns, held subject to his special orders.

To watch his share of the frontier, the Duke disposed the 1st Corps in continuation of the Prussian line about Mons, Enghien, and Nivelles ; the 2nd Corps beyond these points as far west as the line of the Scheldt, the Reserve around Brussels. The Dutch-Belgian cavalry guarded the front of the Prince of

Orange ; some of the King's German hussars did the
same service for Lord Hill ; the rest of the cavalry
were dispersed in cantonments to the rear of the 1st
and 2nd Corps.

These facts are undisputed, and the main question
arising on them is, Whether the whole army of the
Allies, extended thus over a hundred miles of ground
from east to west and forty from north to south,
was not unnecessarily scattered in case of sudden
attack ?   On this important head it is necessary to
point out that Wellington, regarding the defence of
Belgium and of his communications with England
and Germany as objects of first importance, long
afterwards deliberately defended his arrangements.
On the other hand, all Continental critics, looking at
such objects as wholly subsidiary to that of receiving and crushing Napoleon, unanimously condemn
them on this head, Müffling, perhaps, partially excepted.   The latter confesses indeed (as we shall see
presently) that the Prussians do lie under this charge ;
and that, because the case of an attack in the Low
Countries had not been on their side provided for
by the formation of magazines to facilitate concentration.   Time was when it was treasonable to doubt
whether what Wellington arranged was the best
thing possible on his part.   This is not the case now,
however, and we cannot leave this subject without
referring to the deliberate judgment upon it of Sir
S. Kennedy, who has treated it in a complete and
masterly manner.

Supp.
Disp. p.
521.

Müff. Hist.
p. 70.

Kenn. p.
168, *et seq.*

Five great routes, this author points out, presented themselves for the Emperor's choice, and three of these, viz. that by Lille and Ath, that by Mons and Hal, and that by Beaumont, Charleroi, and Genappe, were so ill-watched by the Allied armies that, ' had he advanced by either of them, it is quite clear that it was impossible that they could have been in junction at any point between him and Brussels, so as to have covered it by opposing their united force to him in a general action ; for each of the distances from Liège and Ciney to the nearest parts of the nearest of the three is greater than Napoleon's whole march would be to Brussels. A superficial observer would reply, that they did concentrate in time at Waterloo. But the proposition implies that Napoleon's advance, as supposed, must have compelled the Allies, if they opposed him, to do so without having their whole forces in junction ; and this is what took place [*i.e.* at Quatre Bras and Ligny], and certainly at an imminent risk of being attended with most disastrous results.' Now, the first two of these routes are, with their branches, identical with the roads mentioned by Wellington himself in his Reply to Clausewitz, as necessary for him to observe. Could it have been possible, the question arises, for him to have done this, and to have had Blücher more ready to support him ? This is plainly answered by Kennedy, who was no doubt acquainted with the Duke's defence. He has shown in detail how the armies might have been so disposed when it was heard that the enemy had a large force

Kenn. p. 170.

Supp. Disp. x. 523.

Kenn. p. 172.

organised, that, on his being known to be in motion,
the Prussians might have at once assembled at Genappe and Wellington's troops at Hal. As to the
excuse usually given, the alleged inconvenience as to
supplies, the same critic goes on to dispose of this
very summarily thus : ' In other words, two armies
fully prepared with all their means of taking the field,
in the richest country in Europe, and with their
communications both by sea and land completely
open, were, for this mere supposed inconvenience,
to risk being destroyed in detail by an inferior army.
If the Allied armies had been in this helpless state
as to the means of subsistence, they would have been
totally unequal to manœuvre as an army in junction in face of an enemy.' Thus writes the latest of
the critics who condemn Napoleon without claiming
infallibility for his adversaries. Nor can more be
possibly alleged in their defence than was said by the
earliest of this class, Müffling, whose work appeared
in the full flush of the Allied triumph, and who in
his remarks would willingly exonerate the two Marshals, could he honestly do so, from the charge made
then, and repeated ever since, that they ' were found
by Bonaparte in a situation not prepared to fight ! '
Müff. Hist.
p. 70.
' Wellington, having no other accounts but those of
spies, was unwilling to rely upon them so as to
abandon his principal position for covering Brussels ;
and Blücher, unfortunately, had not the magazines
necessary for concentrating his troops.' Now, Wellington's dispatches sufficiently show that he had

good reasons, some days before the invasion, to be prepared for just such an attack as that which took place, and to expect it to be made by Napoleon himself. Blücher, on German ground, had never shown any special tenderness in gathering supplies for his army, or making the fate of the campaign subservient to the comfort of the territory occupied. We must look elsewhere for a true solution of the quiescent attitude of the Allies ; and it is to be found easily enough by tracing the facts as they occur, which sufficiently prove that Kennedy is strictly just in his broad statement : ' They were not surprised ; they knew of the movements of the French quite in time to have enabled them to assemble their armies before Napoleon passed the frontier. They acted on a different principle, and determined to continue in their cantonments until they knew positively the line of attack. It may safely be predicted that this determination will be considered by future and dispassionate historians as a great mistake ; for in place of waiting to see where the blow actually fell, the armies should have been instantly put in motion to assemble. Nor was this the only error. The line of cantonments occupied was greatly too extended.' With this deliberate opinion we leave the first controversy awakened by our subject, and pass onward to the narrative.

Determined to take the offensive and to take it first in Belgium ; aware that he would be considerably outnumbered by the armies defending that country,

Gur. xii. 449, 457.

See his Reply to a Saxon remonstrance, Ense (2nd ed.) pp. 137, 138.

Kenn. p. 168.

Napoleon had now to decide on the exact line of his operations. The chain of fortresses in his hands would suffice to veil his concentration on any given point of the frontier ; but practically the problem to be solved was not so complicated as this might imply. For reasons already given, the attack could hardly be made on the extreme left of the Allies through the very difficult country which covered it. His choice, therefore, was limited to an advance by his own left near the Scheldt, which would bring him directly upon the communications of Wellington with England, or a movement upon the centre of the Allied line which might, if successful, sever his enemies at least for a time, and enable him to deal with them individually. For the intermediate alternatives of

See Map. throwing himself into the middle of Wellington's cantonments by the line of Valenciennes, or of those of Blücher through the corner of the Ardennes near Namur, promised no special advantage ; and each of them involved the certainty that the greater part of the army attacked would be forced back on that of its ally, and thus oppose superior numbers to the assailant.

This would be of course still more the case if Napoleon chose the first-mentioned plan, and plunged into Belgium by the line of the Scheldt on Wellington's right, thus allowing his enemies to unite for a decisive battle. On the other hand, such a movement might have given him possession of part of the English magazines, and possibly of the capital ; and it

is from such considerations apparently that Welling-
ton, writing his own defence at the age of 72, persisted Supp. Disp. x. 522, 525.
that Napoleon might have made his attack in this
manner with more advantage.   He himself certainly
expected it would thus be made ; and his expectation,
as he himself points out, is abundantly proved by the Ibid. x. 530.
Gurwood Dispatches.   On such a matter few opinions
could be of as great weight ; but Napoleon's is one
of these few, and Napoleon's was very different.
Acting on it he struck at the centre, and although
he failed, the justness of his conception is admitted Cha. p. 80.
by all authorities except Wellington, even by critics Quin. p.75.
who condemn utterly his execution, and charge the Kenn. p. 153.
failure to his own personal shortcomings.

There is a certain square slip of territory lying to
the south of Charleroi, Belgian now (as many authors
on this campaign seem to forget) but French in 1815,
having been wrested originally from the Netherlands
by the victorious Republic of 1794, and confirmed to
France by the easy treaties of 1814 on Napoleon's
first abdication.   Its northern frontier reaches within
six miles of Charleroi.   It is traversed from west to
east by the great road from Maubeuge on the Sambre See Map.
to Givet on the Meuse, which thus makes a large triangle with the courses of these two streams, the apex
being their meeting-point at Namur.   The chief
towns on this road are Beaumont and Philippeville
(the latter an old French fortress which led to the
French claim and possession of the tract), each lying
just fifteen miles from Charleroi to the S.W. and S.E.

respectively. Cross-roads led naturally from each to
the bridges over the Sambre at and near that town :
but these roads, with others near them, had been partly
broken up by Napoleon's order at the beginning of
the Hundred Days for the protection of the French
frontier ; and their bad condition continuing in June

Supp.
Disp.
x. 525.

caused Wellington, in his own words, ' not at first to
give credit to the reports of the intention of the enemy
to attack by the valleys of the Sambre and Meuse.'
No belief could have been more favourable to the
design of his adversary. Once across the Sambre at
Charleroi, Napoleon would have but thirty-four miles
of a first-class chaussée between him and Brussels ;
and, what was still more important, the line of this
great road very nearly coincided with the division of
the country between the two Allied armies. Beaumont and Philippeville were, therefore, designed by
Napoleon as points of assembly for the centre and
right of his army. As Maubeuge is considerably farther from Charleroi than either, the village of Solre,
eight miles lower down the Sambre, but still within
the then French frontier, was the place fixed on for
the starting-point of the left. Though Prussian
troops were known to be quartered to the south of
Charleroi, serious resistance on that side the Sambre
could hardly be expected to the mass Napoleon would
bring ; and it was important to break his army into
these three columns, both for the more convenient
concentration of his troops without confusion and
with the less probability of being observed, as well

as for the more speedy movement of them towards
Charleroi by using a greater number of roads.

It has been said that Napoleon was to lead 128,000
men to his great enterprise. Of this force 22,000
were cavalry and 10,000 artillery ; and the whole
were organised in the manner now traditional in the
Grand Army, the absent ' Fifth Corps ' forming a
separate force upon the Rhine, not disposable for the
Belgian campaign. (It must be understood that the
numbers of each corps are given roundly ; and they
include the detachments of all arms allotted to it,
according to the usual Continental practice.)

1st Corps, D'Erlon	20,000	Thi. xx.23,
2nd ,, Reille	24,500	or (better)
3rd ,, Vandamme . . .	19,000	Cha. p. 56.
4th ,, Gérard	16,000	
6th ,, Lobau	10,500	
Guard	21,000	
Reserve Cavalry, Grouchy . .	13,500	
Train of the army	3,500	
	128,000	

Of these corps the 1st and 2nd were on the open
Belgian frontier, the 3rd near the Ardennes, the 4th
much to the south of this on the Moselle, the 6th,
Guard, and Reserve Cavalry between Belgium and
Paris.   By a simple arrangement as it seems in
theory, a mighty problem to work out in practice,
the 1st and 2nd were closed in quietly to their right
on Solre, forming a left wing ; the 6th marched on
Philippeville, and became the right ; the rest of the

troops were directed on Beaumont. So perfectly was this grand operation timed in hopes of surprising the Cha. p. 55. Allies, that on the night of the 14th the whole army, except a part of the 6th Corps, was lodged quietly in its bivouac close to the Prussian outposts, with orders to keep the watchfires covered by such eminences as were available, and to let no one quit the camps. Sib. i. App. xiii. or App. to Gourg. Elaborate instructions were issued for the advance of the whole at 3 a.m. on the 15th, and the most minute details given for the guidance of the generals, and for the proper arrangement of the baggage. Napoleon loved to commit his ideas on such heads to paper, and, to read these instructions, one might suppose that no mistakes could be made, or would occur, in so well-cared-for an army. Souvenirs de Fezensac, *passim.* But the Duc de Fezensac, in his invaluable ' Souvenirs militaires,' has shown with the utmost plainness that, throughout Napoleon's campaigns, there was a vast and real difference between the paper arrangements and the practical execution. To draw up schemes of commissariat arrangements in a bureau or tent is one thing ; to work them out in the field is quite another. So that if the soldiers of Napoleon's army, on the night of the 14th, were really furnished with the four days' biscuit and half-pound of rice which he intended, and their ammunition pouches properly filled up, it is probably as much as anyone expected to have done or cared to do, judging from such of their former experiences as De Fezensac has revealed.

The movements by which the concentration was

effected may be best studied in their larger features in
the account of M. Thiers.   We need not follow them
out here, since their execution as a whole has never Thi. xx.
17, 19.
been challenged, and for the purpose of the contest the
details are not important.   Yet we shall have occasion, later, to take marked exception to one point in See p. 81.
them.   Students who know the wondrous light thrown
upon other earlier passages of Napoleon's campaigns
by De Fezensac will regret that that faithful observer
and honest loving-hearted critic of the Grand Army
was not present to tell us how far the master's conception was carried out by his workmen, and to give us
a more real insight than novelist or historian has yet
done into the sentiments of officers and men.   Lying
down unsheltered by their watch-fires, as had done
that older Grand Army in which most of them had
served, the 128,000 Frenchmen snatched a few hours'
rest before advancing to the most dangerous adventure their chief had ever launched them on.   To
their right front lay the outposts of Blücher,
covering the cantonments of an army but 10,000
less than theirs.   Not ten miles from the picquets
of Reille and D'Erlon at Solre, began the chain of
Wellington's videttes, behind which nearly 100,000
more combatants were ready at call to support the
Prussians.

It is not only numbers, however, that make an
army formidable.   Its moral and physical power is
composed of many other elements besides, and at this
point we must take a brief survey of some of those

in which the three armies we have to deal with had each their special strength or weakness.

Two of the commanders were still in the prime of life, and in all the apparent vigour of intellect. Whilst Napoleon (arrived from Paris on the 14th at Beaumont) dictated his minute orders for the first movements of the campaign, Wellington's pen was issuing directions not less complicated than his antagonist's. With the same love of detail for which the Emperor was remarkable, he laid down the exact number of muskets and cartridges which were to be put into the petty garrisons of the Belgian frontier, gave precise reasons for refusing a supply of horses to French exiles in arms for the King, and drew up elaborate memoranda for the arrangement of supplies to the Allied armies on the coming general invasion of France. It would be vain to attempt to criticise, within our limits, the previous history of these two greatest of modern generals. The sequel must show how far the powers of execution of each on the field corresponded with, or fell short of, the marvellous fertility of brain in the cabinet which both undoubtedly possessed. The third commander, Blücher, if we admit him to have been somewhat overrated at the time, was yet no ordinary general. He had early in the Revolutionary Wars won special distinction by his constant success in the difficult post of commander of an advance guard, and in the leisure which succeeded this service had drawn up a narrative which still attests the thoroughness of his knowledge of a very

Gur. xii. 464 et seq.

difficult branch of war. Thrown suddenly in 1813 'Blücher's Campagne,' (republished at Hamburg 1866).
into the command of a large army, he had from the
first committed the whole charge of the strategical details to the eminent officers Scharnhorst and
Gneisenau, who filled successively the post of Chief
of Staff, reserving to himself the superintendence of
tactics in actual fight and the control of discipline. His
post was at first no easy one. More than half the force
placed under him consisted of Russian veterans, whose
officers did not conceal their contempt of the young
Prussian recruits who joined them, not their distrust
of the old hussar who was to lead the whole. The
happy victory of the Katzbach, with a frank acknow- Mü. Mem. p. 328.
ledgment of the Russian share in it, made Blücher a
popular commander, and removed all discord from his
motley army, so that, on the crowning day of Leipsic, Ense, p. 245.
he earned his well-known title of ' Marshal *Vorwärts* '
from the Russians of Sacken's corps, who had caught
up from his mouth his favourite word of encouragement, their first lesson in the German tongue. The
coarse, almost brutal language which his staff endured
patiently in consideration of the implicit reliance he Mü. Mem. p. 95, 200.
placed in their judgment, disgusted other officers of
high standing, but not the rough peasants who filled
his battalions. Over these his active personal super-
vision and the familiarity of his address gave him
such power, as no other modern commander but
Napoleon has exercised. Accustomed habitually to
demand from his men more than their utmost exertions Ibid. p. 71.
could perform, this warm feeling towards himself was

often of vital importance, never more so than in this his last campaign. A renowned Marshal, whose men, as he rode by an advancing column, would grasp his knee joyfully with the soldier's salutation, 'Good work to-day, father,' might at times press these men on when another would have failed. The will of the soldier is a more potent element in the combinations of war than military writers generally admit. If love for his general be needful for controlling it, Blücher had called this faculty out with no less success than Napoleon ; whilst in the army of Wellington it took no higher form than respect for his great powers. A stringent discipline for the men, and a fine sense of duty among the officers, might go far to supply the want with the veteran British troops ; and through the whole heterogeneous mass the knowledge of their leader's long career of victory could not but help to break the spell of invincibility which still clung to the name of Napoleon. Yet, to a candid judgment, the Englishman appears in this regard far behind both his ally and his great rival.

Ense, p. 186.

Of the chief lieutenants of the latter it is necessary to say a few words. Partly for their real soldierly qualities, partly because so long held up to the world by virtue of their master's fame, most of them have made historic names. Soult, who filled the post of Chief of Staff, was a soldier of such established reputation, that it would not be necessary to enlarge upon it, were it not that M. Thiers tries to fasten upon him part of the blame of the Waterloo disaster, and charges him beforehand with a want of that clearness Thi. xx.30. and experience which such a post demands. This is not the only place in which the historian appears imbued with the old political animosity of the debates in the Chambers of Louis Philippe. It is enough here to note that the charges made rest generally for their proof upon an alleged inferiority in Soult's way of carrying out the Emperor's wishes as compared to that of Berthier. We shall have occasion to look to this matter in detail at the proper time. Ney and Grouchy had also made European reputations in their profession—reputations constantly maintained ever since they were first won in the old campaigns of Jourdan and Moreau. The former was about to join, but not yet present; the latter had from the first been chosen by Napoleon to lead his reserve cavalry for his eminent services in the previous year. There is no proper foundation in history for the statement of Thiers, that he only obtained this because neither Ibid. p. 21. Murat, Bessières, Montbrun, nor Lasalle were at hand, save the fact that *the first two* had stood before him in Napoleon's favour. Thiers, using their names, has appended to them two others of lesser rank, and, by assuming Grouchy inferior to the whole, would lower him beforehand in the reader's estimate. Of the other generals, Reille and D'Erlon had left the Peninsula with high reputations, the former having made a glorious name at Vittoria, where his conduct saved the débris of Joseph's army from destruction. Vandamme had been a true ' man of war,' in Napoleon's favourite phrase, having been constantly serving in command of troops ever since he led a division in this same Belgian district, twenty-two years before, against the Duke of York. Lobau had been long ago distinguished for cool daring surpassing that of other men, even in an army where such conduct, with moderate ability for command, was the short road to rank and fortune. Gérard was younger than these in his high post, having been little known until the Russian campaign, but had, from his first promotion to a division, been a man of mark in the Grand Army. He justified Napoleon's choice long after in high office under the monarchy, and to him it fell to lead, with England's approval, another French army into Belgium, and to divide that very kingdom of the Netherlands, to protect which Waterloo was nominally fought.

The Imperial Guard had no head in this campaign, Marshal Mortier having fallen sick upon the frontier, and there being no one of sufficient rank to take the chief control of that jealous corps. Napoleon, as we shall see towards the close, has made full use of this mishap in his attempts to excuse his disaster.

Many of the division generals in the French army were men of real eminence in their profession. Kellermann had done Napoleon service of the highest order at Marengo, and had quite as much claim to respect as a cavalry general as Montbrun and Lasalle, put by Thiers before Marshal Grouchy. Foy, originally an artillery officer, had shown his great ability a hundred times in the long Peninsular struggle, as he lived to prove it afterwards as a writer and orator. The school of Napoleon had many faults, but, on the whole, no army was probably ever so well furnished with leaders as his, as none had ever the like experience wherewith to train them.

The Prussian chiefs of corps were hardly men of the same high mark as the French. Bülow, indeed, must be excepted, for he had held a weightier post, had commanded armies, and won an important victory. But Zieten, Pirch, and Thielemann were little known except as good division generals. It was not then generally understood, nor have French or English writers shown how it came about, that these important charges were in their hands, when leaders so distinguished in 1813 as York, Kleist, and Tauenzein were not far off. Blücher's uncertain health and the desire of the King that Gneisenau should succeed him in case of accident, were the real causes. Hard work and hard living had told upon the iron frame of the old hussar, who (according to the Russian historian Danilewski) had at times broken down completely in the spring of the previous year. But the fiery trials of the revolutionary wars had not purged from the Prussian army the spirit of excessive reverence for seniority which ruled even the royal will ; and in case, therefore, of Blücher's falling ill, the command could only devolve on Gneisenau by means of the previous removal of all other generals older in rank than that

For all this see Mü. Mem. p. 227.

officer. This was accordingly done, with the exception of Bülow, whose corps was to form a reserve in Belgium, whilst the rest moved on to Paris in July. This elaborate arrangement was nullified by Napoleon's attack, but it serves sufficiently to show how little that attack had been expected in the beginning.

Wellington's 1st and 2nd Corps were commanded, Ante, p.42, Table. as before seen, by the Prince of Orange and Lord Hill, an arrangement strongly indicating the conflict of diplomatic and military elements in all the arrangements of the English general at that busy epoch. The Prince had seen Peninsular service as an aide-de-camp. His royal birth and the hereditary courage of his house were his only other claims to his post. Lord Hill, on the contrary, had, through many years of warfare, proved himself beyond dispute a worthy lieutenant of his great chief, whether acting in his sight or in detached command. The Reserve Corps Wellington gave no head to, whether despising the more finished organisation created under Napoleon,* or whether really doubtful of the capacity of his other generals. Of these it would be invidious here to say more than that Picton alone has left a name known beyond the limits of national history, and the fame of this gallant officer probably owes something of its freshness to his death upon the field of victory. Edin. Rev. 1862. At the time we are writing of he was out of favour

Mémoires de St. Cyr, ii. 114.

* Moreau, the first modern general to employ corps d'armée, kept his Reserve Corps under his own command, causing (as St. Cyr informs us) much jealousy on the part of the others.

with Wellington.   We are assured by an eye-witness of apparent credibility that, at their last meeting, the only one of the campaign, the field-marshal showed this feeling unmistakably before his staff.

As concerns material, each army was fairly provided. Napoleon had the greater number of guns (344), but the Prussians not many less (312).   The supply in the Anglo-allied army was as much smaller as those would expect who knew how Wellington had, in previous years, complained of our scanty provision of this important arm : it amounted in total to 196, all told, and of these one important part, the 18-pounders, or ' guns of position ' for the reserve, were never brought into the field.   Critics of the day, whose remarks have since passed out of sight, did not fail to discover this absence, and comment unfavourably on it. Müffling in his earlier work has explained rather than justified the fact, in words which go to confirm the proofs that the Allied arrangements had, up to June, been made chiefly upon the false hypothesis that they were not to be attacked. ' The Duke of Wellington's not having his 18-pounders in the battle may probably be the consequence of an agreement on our part, not to commence offensive operations until the 1st of July. That artillery, therefore, either had not been organised or not brought up from Antwerp in time to appear at the battle.   Upon the rise behind La Haye Sainte it would have been of extraordinary service to the Duke of Wellington on the 18th.'

These heavy guns, though forming three batteries,

Müff. Hist. p. 83.

Sib.i.App. vi. numbered only twelve.   Deducted from Wellington's armament, they leave him with but 184 to take the field, little more than half the supply that Napoleon had got together, and less than two-thirds of his ally's.   On the other hand, his proportion of cavalry (over 14,000) was greater than that (12,000) of Blücher, whilst Napoleon had taken special pains to attain strength in this arm, and could count on 22,000 horsemen, a number nearly equal to those of Cha. p. 58. his enemies united.   By using them freely he doubtless hoped to improve any success obtained at the first onset.   On the other hand, the French army was proportionably weak in the mainstay of battle, containing not quite 90,000 infantry, less than half of the 181,000 Sib. i. App. vi. Cha. p. 69. of that arm which the Allies had gathered in the Netherlands.

Numbers are, as before remarked, but an uncertain test of the weight of an army.   Above all other elements, this depends on the goodness of the individual soldiers, and in this matter the Emperor had an advantage which no writer will now-a-days dispute.   It was no mass of conscripts that he led into Belgium.   The raw youths who had first seen fire at Lutzen in 1813 had perished in the terrible campaigns that followed before the first Abdication, or had hardened perforce into valuable soldiers.   One-third of the new Grand Army was of these 'novices of 1813 and 1814,' as Thi. xx.21. M. Thiers calls them, who admits that, of the whole host, there was not a man that had not served before ; for the remaining two-thirds had come back returned

from distant prisons in Germany or Russia, veterans
of as high order as the school of Napoleon could produce. Speaking one tongue, holding one creed of
military loyalty, inspired with ' not merely patriotism
or enthusiasm, but an actual passion against their
enemies,' if we make every possible deduction for the
high colouring of national historians, it may still be
assumed that no such compactly formidable mass of
troops ever moved into the field before.

    The Prussian army, though of no less fierce and
dangerous a spirit, was far inferior in the quality of
its men. Nearly one-half of its infantry and cavalry
were landwehr, hastily trained under the new system
introduced by Scharnhorst during the period of French
supremacy. Of the regular troops a large proportion
were recruits, for the exhausting campaigns which had
carried their standards from the Oder to the Seine
had made large gaps among the enthusiastic volun-
teers that filled the regiments in 1813. Veterans and
recruits, however, were alike of one tongue and one
race, and moved by the same patriotic ardour. They
were, as before said, not behind the French in love for
their general, the living representative of the late
glorious resurrection of their country ; and with him
they burned to punish the usurper who had but lately
trampled her under his heel of iron, and whose ambition now once more brought the curse of war on
Europe. Woe to the legions of Napoleon, it might
have been predicted, should they flee before enemies
so fierce and relentless as these.

Foy's
Journal
quoted.
Thi. xx.
21 n.

When we pass from such armies as those of Napoleon and Blücher, to examine the motley mass under Wellington, we cannnot wonder at the contempt with which its chief spoke of it in various letters. Mr.

Hooper, p. 36.

Hooper has quoted aptly from the best known of these, and especially the reference of the Duke to the small numbers of his British. But the real estimate made by Wellington of the comparative fighting means

Gur. xii. 438.

of the two Allied armies has escaped most writers. It is to be found in a letter of the 2nd June, in which he expressly calculates the number of men with which the Prussians were to invade France as ' twice as many ' as his own. Yet his force was nearly equal to Blücher's in number ; and even if we reckon with the Prussians a corps of 20,000 Germans on the Moselle, it would be but a quarter less. Of Wellington's 106,000, however, barely one-third were British ; and of this a good part recruits mixed with his Peninsular veterans, or in new battalions hastily raised ; whilst ranking lower than even these last in worth were garrison battalions not intended for field service. There were some thousands of King's Germans, raised long since, chiefly in Hanover, and hardened into veterans of the first order by years of successful war ; with four times as many Hanoverian recruits, formed mostly into landwehr regiments, in hasty imitation of the Prussian system. Good service might be expected from the Brunswickers, led by their Duke, descendant of a line of warlike ancestors, and noted beyond other princes of Germany for his patriotic ardour :

but the Nassau Contingent, newly raised in the Rhine
country but lately wrested from the Empire, was
considered of more doubtful value. As to the troops
of the Netherlands, whose numbers nearly equalled
the British, the lack of sympathy between their two
chief elements, the Dutch and Belgian, was notorious ;
and all had been long accustomed to bear the French
yoke, and believe in the spell of Napoleon's name. In
this single portion of Wellington's force were men of
three different races ; for the House of Orange had
claims in Nassau, had raised troops in that country,
and had in its pay a whole brigade of such Germans,
a body now lying on the extreme left of Wellington's
cantonments, and therefore the first of his army to
come to blows with the advancing enemy. The following table, founded on Siborne's returns, gives a
vivid idea of the heterogeneous composition of the
mass termed in those days the *English* Army by
writers of other nations :—

Sib. i. App. vi.

See Gourgaud ; Blücher's Report ; Austrian Report.

Table of Forces under Wellington.

(1) British Field Force 33,709
(2) British Garrison Battalions 2,017
(3) King's German Legion 6,387
(4) Hanoverian Levies embodied in British Divisions 15,935
(5) Hanoverian Levies recently arrived . . . 9,000
(6) Brunswick Contingent 6,808
(7) Nassau 2,880
(8) Dutch and Belgian Troops 24,914
(9) Nassauers in Dutch Service 4,300

                                             105,950

F

Of these, we know that (2) and (5), making 11,000 men, were not fitted for the field, and that there were serious suspicions of the fidelity to the Allied cause of the 32,000 comprehended in (7), (8), and (9). Very probably these suspicions were in some degree unjust and exaggerated ; but that they existed is undeniable, and they must have inevitably affected the plans of Wellington, as we have shown they did his estimate of his moveable numbers. Napoleon may be justified in reckoning the armies he attacked as each numerically nearly equal to his own ; but one of them was inferior in training, and from the other's nominal strength large deductions were to be made. By so much, therefore, was his rashness redeemed from the reproach of daring the impossible.

Gourg. pp. 31, 33.

We left the Emperor in bivouac with his army waiting for the daylight of the 15th. ' The Allied armies,' he tells us, ' remained in perfect security in their cantonments ; ' but this is a mere French guess at the other side, and, for reasons already given, we must go to the historians of that side to know the truth. Taking Müffling's narrative as that of the man whose special business it was to know what went on at each Allied headquarters, we find that, ' on the 13th and 14th, it was positively known that the enemy was concentrating in the neighbourhood of Maubeuge. The Duke of Wellington [acting under the expectation commented on before] did not deem it expedient to make any alteration in his position, until the enemy should further develop his mode of attack, as from

Ibid. p. 31.

Müff. Hist. Intro.

See ante, pp. 44, 50.

Maubeuge it might be either upon Mons, Binche, and Nivelles, or upon Charleroi.' Blücher was not so patient. The precautions which Napoleon thought successful had in fact failed to blind the videttes of Zieten before Charleroi. As the Prussian narrative Pr. Off. p. 7. puts it, with a touch of life not often to be found in its dry pages, ' Whoever has once campaigned cannot fail to know that fires of this sort lighting up the whole atmosphere are seen far enough off, and render this kind of precaution very useless. So in this case the fires were distinctly noted from the Prussian outposts.' As early as the night of the 13th, Zieten had Ibid. p. 9. reported the gathering of two great camps at Beaumont and Solre, and had been ordered to send his heavy baggage off towards Gembloux. Further reports from this officer, obtained by observation and through fugitives crossing the frontier, were sent to Blücher on the 14th; and, late that evening, the Marshal's orders went out to the Prussian corps. Zeiten was to fall back and hold Fleurus, a small Ibid. pp. 9, 20. country town seven miles north-east of Charleroi; the other three to concentrate preparatory to a general march on the same place.

So passed the short night which preceded Napoleon's last campaign : * the French, impatient for the

* *Note on the state of Napoleon's health in* 1815.—Certain French writers, among whom it is painful to number Charras, are disposed to impute a large share of their country's disaster to some supposed falling off of the physical energy and mental powers of the Emperor. The simple reply to this is, that his warlike capacity had never been more splendidly displayed than during that part of the struggle with the Allies of the spring of 1814, known as the Week of Victories.

light in which to fall upon their foes, and redeem, by
some new Austerlitz or Jena, the disasters of the last
three years ; the Prussians, no less vigilant, preparing
in all haste to meet the shock ; the English, save
only their reticent chief and a few trusted officers,
resting unconscious of the gathering storm before
them.

The general of Arcola and Rivoli was not more full of resource, nor
more sudden and deadly in his strokes, than he of Montmirail and
Champaubert.   As to his actual health during the campaign of
Waterloo, Thiers (*vide* vol. xx. p. 59) has devoted a valuable note
to the subject, and sufficiently shown that he was physically capable
of fully bearing the fatigues incident to a bold aggressive campaign.
Were this excuse worth employing, we may be sure the great French
advocate would not have been at the pains of demolishing it.

LECTURE III.

EVENTS OF THE 15TH JUNE.—COMMENTS.—SUMMARY.

THE first day of the campaign broke fair on the expectant French. The evening previous there had been read from regiment to regiment one of those stirring proclamations with which Napoleon had been wont, ever since he first held a command, to herald his important operations. The orders to the corps, sent out before the light, prescribed the movement of the left and centre to begin at 3 a.m., and Gérard's from the right at the same hour, ' provided [let this be noted] his divisions were together.' Thiers, whose readers have been told that the Allied generals suspected ' nothing, or next to nothing, of the French designs,' here goes on to say that, at the appointed hour, the whole army moved, excepting Vandamme, and gives no hint that Napoleon himself doubted Gérard's being ready. In truth the early movement began only with the left, where Reille, who had lain in front of Solre, went off at the appointed hour, following a road down the right bank of the Sambre, which crosses the river at the bridge of Marchiennes, two miles above Charleroi, and soon coming into

Gour. App. (' Ordre, &c.')p.142, Thi. xx. 27.

Ibid. p. 29.

collision with the Prussian posts near Thuin. By ten

Cha. p. 84. they were forced back beyond Marchiennes, and the bridge (which Zieten had neglected to mine) was in Ibid. p. 86. French hands. Gérard had been detained until 5 a.m., waiting for the rear of his corps to come in. The centre of the army (comprising Vandamme, Lobau, the Guards and Reserve Cavalry), though lying the nearest to Napoleon's own headquarters, was the last of the three columns to put its head in motion north-ward. Vandamme's corps lay in front, and Van-damme had had no orders ! The solitary officer who bore them had fallen on the way, and been badly hurt, and Vandamme lay tranquilly in bivouac until Lobau's corps, which had started at four, came up, and the state of things was with difficulty explained. The Ibid. App. D. story has been told just as it happened, by Colonel Janin, of Lobau's staff, who shows that Vandamme was moved on by this pressure on his rear, and not, Thi. xx.30. as Thiers inaccurately states, by the urging of the General of Engineers who was with him. This differ-ence matters little, for the fact remains admitted, that the advance of the whole mass of the centre was made dependent on the punctual arrival of a single messenger. Pajol, whose cavalry corps (one of the four embodied in the Reserve) had been placed in front of Vandamme, had gone on unsupported, and though he forced the Prussian posts to retire on Charleroi, his horsemen could not carry the bridge at that town in face of the Prussian rearguard. It was Doc. 141. noon, according to the bulletin issued (half-past ten, by the St. Helena version), when Pajol passed through Gourg.
p. 37. the town, the bridge having been carried by the marines and sappers of the Guard who preceded Van- Cha. p. 8
Hooper,
p. 70. damme. According to some accounts (as Charras', whom Hooper appears here to follow), the retreat of the Prussians was forced by the arrival of the Young Guard, hurried up by a side road under the direction of Napoleon himself. But the Emperor's own state- ment in his original narrative was, that the entry into Gourg.
p. 37. Charleroi was made half an hour before he reached the bridge, and on such a point we must believe him to be right.

Whilst the bridges of Marchiennes and Charleroi were thus both in French hands at noon, after a delay at the latter, reckoned by Napoleon at four hours, and Ibid. called by him ' un funeste contretems,' Gérard had not yet gained the river. He had started, as has been seen, at 5 a.m. ; but his columns were not long on the road (being directed like the centre on Charleroi), when the news spread through the corps that the general of its leading division, Bourmont, had basely deserted to the enemy. This was indeed true, and the fact afforded too good a pretext for subsequent misfor- tune not to be made use of by the St. Helena pen, and the crowd of writers who have followed it. By these Ibid.
p. 34, &c. the 14th has been generally assigned as the day of the desertion, which, it is implied, must have been of special use to the Allies in revealing Napoleon's ad- vance. Thiers found this story exploded when he Thi. xx. 56. wrote, and has corrected it emphatically, as indeed he

could not help doing after the publication of the note
Cha. p.
87, n.
on the subject by Charras, who has fully proved the
truth from the Paris archives.   Possibly the desertion
caused a halt during the necessary report to Napoleon.
The only certainty in the matter is, that an order
Gourg.
p. 142.
reached Gérard subsequently to that originally given,
directing him to march on the bridge of Châtelet, four
miles to the east of Charleroi, and below it on the
river, which he only reached late in the day.   The rear
of his column had had more than twenty miles to
Thi. xx.54.
Cha. p. 98.
march over bad roads, and half his corps did not cross
the stream that night, though the Prussians had here
also left the bridge intact, and made no resistance.
He may be left out of sight, therefore, from the rest of
the operations of the day.

The great road from Charleroi to Brussels runs, as
before said, nearly due north.   At the point now
Ferrari's
Map, 1770.
known as Quatre Bras (but called Trois Bras in old
maps), which is thirteen miles from Charleroi and
twenty-one from Brussels, it crosses another chaussée
running from Nivelles eastward to Namur.   Another
See Map
accom-
panying.
main road leaves it just out of Charleroi, and, passing
by Fleurus, strikes at a like distance from the former
place the same Namur-Nivelles road at Sombreffe,
eight miles east from Quatre Bras.   That point, with
Sombreffe and Charleroi, marks thus a triangular piece
of ground, which we shall call the Fleurus triangle, of
vital importance to Napoleon's future operations, the
Namur-Nivelles road being the chief communication
between the Allied armies.   Long since the English

and Prussian chiefs had recognised this, and the danger of their being separated, should the French seize that road at Quatre Bras and Sombreffe. At a meeting held by them at Tirlemont on the 3rd May, they had discussed the possibility of the enemy's advance through Charleroi in such an attempt to sever their armies, and had agreed as to the movements to be undertaken to counteract so dangerous an attack. The reasons for these are fully given by Müffling, and it is sufficient to say here that, in the given case, the Prussian army was to assemble between Sombreffe and Charleroi, the English between Marchiennes and Gosselies, a village on the Charleroi-Brussels road, four miles from the former place, and the junction-point of a cross-road from the Sambre at Marchiennes. Had these positions been attained, the Allied armies would have nearly touched, and have guarded all the approaches from the Sambre into the Fleurus triangle, so that whichever one Napoleon attacked would be aided by a flank attack upon him by the other. Such were the Allied views beforehand. Yet, at 3 p.m. on the 15th, but one Prussian corps was near the ground, and saving one division (Perponcher's Dutch Belgians), not a man of Wellington's army within reach of it, whilst the head of a column of 40,000 Frenchmen had passed the Sambre at Marchiennes, and that of another of nearly 70,000 was entering Charleroi !

Reille (whose account Charras here follows) had defiled across the river and taken post halfway between Marchiennes and Gosselies, when Napoleon made his

Gur. xii. 345. Mü. Mem. p. 231.

Ibid. p. 232.

Cha. p. 88.

For de-
tails, Pr.
Off. p. 13.
own way out of Charleroi.   At this time about 10,000 of Zieten's troops were towards Gosselies under General Steinmetz, the rest retiring in the direction of Fleurus, but showing a good front.   It needed a considerable deployment of Reille's troops in front of Gosselies before the Prussians there were dislodged and

Ibid. p. 14,
and Bul-
letin. Doc.
141.
retired across on Fleurus, leaving the road to Quatre Bras open.   Napoleon himself had to take command in a more severe combat on the Sombreffe road along

Gourg.
p. 42.
which Vandamme and Grouchy were directed ; for they had hesitated to act in his absence against Zieten,

Ibid. p. 57.
whose rearguard fronted them boldly halfway between Charleroi and Fleurus.   He had been unwilling to ride on to that side until he knew that Reille was able to occupy Gosselies and secure his left, and thus the French had lost two hours more.   Thanks to their mistakes and his own firmness, Zieten, though unsupported, actually held possession of Fleurus at dark, keeping some wood to the south of it with his advance guard, but having his corps mostly on the other side nearer to the Namur-Nivelles road, where he occupied the heights about the village of Bry, since known as the hill of Ligny.

Before leaving the point where the road to Fleurus turned off, and taking personal command in this skirmish, Napoleon received a reinforcement to his staff in the person of Ney, known as ' the bravest of the brave ' in the Grand Army, as he had been distinguished long before any Grand Army was formed.

Cha. p. 89.
Thi. xx. 41.
After some words of welcome from the Emperor, he

was at once invested with the charge of the left column (some cavalry being added for his use to the corps of Reille and D'Erlon), and received certain verbal orders the tenor of which is much disputed, but which implied a present advance upon the Brussels road.   The Prussians were now quitting this, under Reille's pressure, carrying of course with them, in their movement on Fleurus, all the detachments which had connected their right with the outposts on the English left that morning, and leaving the direct line to Brussels open as far as they were concerned.   Ney followed up Steinmetz with a single division (Girard's) of Reille's corps, as soon as he had fairly assumed the command assigned to him.   Another division of infantry (Bachelu's), preceded by one of cavalry (Piré's), was directed towards Quatre Bras.   Reille's two remaining divisions were posted in reserve at Gosselies.   With the Guard cavalry left him by Napoleon, Ney soon followed Bachelu and Piré in their northward march.   Before, however, he had overtaken them they had met the first troops seen by the French of Wellington's army, who were posted in the village of Frasnes, two miles from Quatre Bras.   The Dutch brigade of Nassauers had been quartered that morning along the Brussels road from Frasnes northward to Genappe, five miles nearer to Brussels.   An accident to the brigadier had that day placed the command in the hands of the senior colonel, the young Prince Bernard of Saxe Weimar; and he, becoming aware of the advance of the French on Charleroi, had drawn together his brigade, at Quatre

Cha. p. 90.
Thi. xx.44.

Thi. xx.44.

Ante, p.69.

Vide his letter,Doc. 85 (or in Supp. Disp. X., where it is repub- lished).

P.
Orange's
Report,
Doc. 86.

Bras, leaving one battalion and a light battery at Frasnes in advance. It was the guns of the latter which had fired on Ney's cavalry; and, although the outposts soon retired on their main body at Quatre Bras, Prince Bernard prepared to hold the cross-roads at the latter place. Ney on his arrival reconnoitred. The ground rising up for 500 yards towards Quatre Bras served to conceal the real strength of the Prince's force, which was also covered partly by a wood that in those days filled the south-eastern angle of the cross-roads. It was now 8 p.m. and nearly

Ibid.

dark. Ney could not know how many troops he had before him; but his own men had been on the march for seventeen hours, and were, as he must have known from the last dropping shots near Fleurus, considerably in advance of the main body of the

Cha. p. 91.
Thi. xx. 47.

army. He made no attempt, therefore, to take ground beyond Frasnes, and, leaving there the troops he had brought up, returned to Gosselies, and later to visit Napoleon, who had gone back to Charleroi for the night.

Thi. xx. 54.
Cha. p. 94,
&c.

The French lay thus. On the left, most of Ney's cavalry and one division of Reille's infantry held Frasnes; two more infantry divisions were at Gosselies. The fourth (Girard's) had left this column and now lay not far from Fleurus, at the village of Wangenies, touching the troops of Grouchy and Vandamme. D'Erlon had crossed the Sambre, and his corps was posted on the first portion of the cross-road leading from Marchiennes to Gosselies. In the centre the

infantry of the Guard had got to Charleroi, but their
heavy cavalry, with two of Grouchy's four reserve
corps and Lobau's corps, bivouacked on the south side
of the Sambre. So did one half of Gérard's corps,
which had not been up in time to cross at Châtelet.
35,000 men, at the least computation, had not yet Thi. xx.27.
got over the stream. Yet the order of the day told the
generals explicitly, that the 'design of his Majesty Gourg.
p. 144.
was to have crossed (*est d'avoir passé*) before noon,
and to carry the army to the left bank of the river.'
So much easier is it in war to design than to execute,
and to move a staff than to transport the bulk of an
army.

Of the Prussians, the story for this day is easily
told. News of the attack on Zieten had been dis- Pr. Off.
p. 17.
patched to Blücher at break of day, and it may be
supposed that the Marshal did not the less hurry on
the two corps which had lain nearest his headquarters
at Namur the night before. By dark Pirch had halted
at Mazy, four miles from Sombreffe, on the road from
Namur, and Thielemann's corps had reached the latter
place, being ten miles farther off. Two hours' march
would bring the former general, and five the latter, on
the ground already taken by Zieten before Ligny,
and their orders were to press on at daybreak. With
Bülow the case was very different. This general,
whose corps had been much farther from headquarters,
received his first orders only at 5 a.m. on the
15th. These were to concentrate his troops *so as to* Ibid. p. 18.
be able to get to Hannut (the chief place on the direct

road from Liège across to Sombreffe) *in a day's
march*. This operation was in course of execution
when, at 10.30 a.m., he received a second order, dated
at midnight, ordering a movement on Hannut. As
some of his troops could not be informed of this until

Pr. Off.

late in the afternoon, and as Gneisenau's letter made
no mention of actual hostilities, he put off the execution of these second instructions till next day, promising to be at Hannut by noon of the 16th. But
Hannut is full twenty-five miles from Ligny, where
his presence was sorely needed ere that hour was
long passed.

Ibid.
p. 17.

According to Zieten's own statement he had dispatched a courier to Wellington at 4 a.m. to say that
he was attacked in force. His staff service must have
been but poorly arranged, since the officer who bore
this important news did not reach Müffling until

Mü. Mem.
p. 271.

3 p.m., having taken apparently eleven hours to
traverse a distance which an ordinary pedestrian might
have covered in the same time. Wellington had at
that hour received no intelligence from his own posts
about Mons under General Dornberg ; but there was

Supp.
Disp. XII.
524.

with him the Prince of Orange, who had left his own
headquarters and come up to report—although in very
vague language—the early attack on Thuin of which

Mü. Mem.
p. 272.

he had heard. After some discussion with Müffling,
the Duke explained, that, as he could not yet know the
right point for concentration (the French design not
being developed fully), he should content himself for
the present with ordering all the troops to be in

readiness.   This was soon after done, though at what
exact hour is not agreed on.*   Of the Prince of
Orange's corps, the first and third British divisions
were to collect at Ath and Braine-le-Comte respectively, and the two Dutch-Belgian divisions
(Chassé's and Perponcher's) at Nivelles.   The 3rd
British division was directed also to march on Nivelles
'should that point have been attacked this day,' but
'not until it is quite certain the enemy's attack is upon
the right of the Prussian and the left of the British
army.'   At the hour when this was written, Prince
Bernard had already concentrated his brigade at
Quatre Bras, as we have seen, and his proceeding was
fully approved by an order dispatched from Braine-le-
Comte in the Prince of Orange's absence by his chief
of staff, Constant Rebecque, to General Perponcher, to
whose division Bernard belonged.   This directed the
general to put his troops under arms, *keeping one
brigade at Quatre Bras*, and the other at Nivelles.   In
accordance with these instructions, Bernard was left in
the position he had taken up for the night, and the
other brigade under Bylandt, at Nivelles.   The Prince
of Orange remained at Brussels with Wellington, and
accompanied him to the famous ball, after a second

Mü Mem.
Sib. i. 71.
Hooper,
p. 81.
Cha.p.109.

Gur. x.
472.

See Orig.
Loben S.
p. 128.

* In his Reply to Clausewitz (Supp. Disp. XII. 524), the Duke
says, ' Orders were forthwith sent *for the march of the whole army to
its left* ;' but this is manifestly in advance of the facts, as is shown
by all other testimony. It is, for instance, contradicted explicitly by
Siborne's and Hooper's narratives.   The *first* orders, indeed (to
make ready), were sent out 'at once' according to Siborne, 'about
5 p.m.' by Hooper, 'about 6 or 7 p.m.' by Müffling. Charras, on
the testimony of the Dutch archives, makes it later.

Or Gleig's
' Brial.' ii.
App.

order—the order of movement—had been dispatched
to the troops.   This was the result of a decisive report
from Mons, that the enemy had turned on Charleroi
with all his forces, and that there were no troops before
the former place.   But Wellington's subordinates,
better informed than their chief, were again beforehand
with him.   Constant Rebecque had been fully acquainted at 10 p.m. with the affair at Quatre Bras, and
had warned Perponcher to support Prince Bernard
with the rest of his division.   He reported this proceeding and its cause at the same time to the Prince of
Orange; and although Perponcher afterwards received,
through Rebecque, Wellington's first order from
Brussels, *to collect at Nivelles*, he adhered—as was
natural with his knowledge of the circumstances—to
the previous one, and found his resolve approved by
the Prince, who reached Braine from Brussels before
3 a.m., having been treated with some petulance by
Wellington for his display of anxiety as to the advance
of the French against his corps.

Wellington's second orders for the British divisions,
issued as he went to the ball, were simple.   The 3rd
British division was now to move on Nivelles ; the
1st to follow it to Braine.   The two under Lord Hill
(2nd and 4th) were to follow the movement eastward,
and march on Enghien.   The cavalry reserve was
directed on the last place.   Prince Frederic's Dutch-
Belgians had already been ordered, through Lord Hill,
to collect at Sotteghem, and had no further instructions
till the afternoon of the 16th.   No alteration was as

Mü. Mem.
p. 230.

See Orig.
Loben S.
p. 176.

Ibid.

Edin. Rev.
1862.

Gur. x.
474.

yet made in the dispositions directing Chassé and Per- Loben S. p. 181.
poncher to gather at Nivelles ; and the division of
Dutch-Belgian cavalry, under Collaert, was to move
from near Mons to Arquennes, a village close to the
former town.   The movements were ' to take place
with as little delay as possible,' and began with the
troops near Brussels (of whom we have not yet spoken)
soon after daybreak.   All this pointed plainly to a
concentration on Nivelles, and, if carried out literally,
would have left Quatre Bras and the road towards
Brussels for some miles open to Ney.   For some miles Gur. x. 472, and Duenes.
only, because the Reserve Corps, held in readiness from
the evening before under Wellington's own eye, was
put in motion at daybreak by his direction, and
marched towards Waterloo.   From this point (where See Chap. IV. 'Com- ments.'
the leading British division was halted on the 16th for
some hours) Wellington could direct it on Nivelles or
Quatre Bras as he judged fittest.   The short night was Sib. i. 102.
passed, however, without a man of his army having
moved towards the enemy, save those Dutch-Belgians
who had concentrated without his orders.

Comments.

It has been said before, that exception may be Ante,p.52.
taken in one point to the details of Napoleon's concentration.   Fine as it undoubtedly was, the absolute perfection claimed for it by his admirers disappears when
it is shown, from the words of his own *ordre du mouve-* Ante, p.69.
ment (already quoted), and the admission of Thiers, Thi. xx.54.
that Gérard's corps was not wholly brought up on the

14th.   Half a day's march gained on the way from
Metz would have left that general as ready to start on
the 15th as was Reille, and enabled him to arrive at
midday at Châtelet, put all his troops over the bridge
there left him, and, connecting his advance with Vandamme's as the latter passed out of Charleroi, to drive

Gourg.
p. 58.
Zieten, thus completely outflanked, at once beyond
Fleurus.   In his earliest and most genuine account,
Napoleon expressly gives the continued occupation of
that place by the Prussians as the reason that Ney did
not advance to Quatre Bras that night.   If there be
any truth in this, the delay of Gérard, whose bridge
was but two miles from the left flank of the position in
which the Prussians checked Vandamme, has a more
serious bearing on the affairs of the day than has been

Claus.
p. 57.
hitherto assigned it.   Clausewitz does not comment on
it specially, but his narrative sets in the clearest light
the advantage which accrued to Zieten from the two
hours' pause of the French in his front.   That Zieten
was thus exposed to this contingency seems, however,
to be in some degree that general's own fault.   No
satisfactory explanation has been ever given of the
reasons of his allowing the bridges, which were left on
his flanks as he quitted Charleroi, to fall into the
enemy's hands unmined and without resistance.   The
information which he himself sent off to the Allied
generals proves clearly that he was not blind to the
coming danger, and it does not appear why he took so
little pains to prepare for its approach.

The delay of Vandamme's corps, and by it of the

whole centre, is in every way more striking and im- Mém. ix. 77.
portant. In the 'Mémoires' Napoleon has asserted
roundly that his plan was this day perfectly carried out;
and that, although not advanced to Fleurus, his army
'already found itself placed between the Prussians and
English, and able to turn on either of them. All its
manœuvres had succeeded to the full.' But his former
narrative contradicts this effectually. The expression Gourg. p. 37.
applied to Vandamme's delay, 'un funeste contretems,'
can certainly not form any part of these fully successful
manœuvres. Moreover, Napoleon in another part of Mém. ix. 159.
the same volume of the 'Mémoires' says of the delay
of this day, 'This loss of seven hours was very unfortunate.' Thiers goes much further than Napoleon Thi. xx. 43.
in speaking of the mishap. He accepts the Emperor's
assertion (made in a reply to General Rogniat's stric- Mém. viii. 196.
tures) that Vandamme's advance on Fleurus was not
really desirable ; omits to note that this is directly con- See Note at page 93.
tradicted by Napoleon's own expressions just quoted;
and, desiring to leave no loss to be borne by the mere
mischance of a contretemps, he deliberately charges
the fault of Vandamme's delay on Soult's omission to Thi. xx. 30.
follow Berthier's habit, and send a duplicate and tripli-
cate of the order. As the historian in two other Ibid. 65, 266.
places refers to this supposed incapacity of Soult for
his special duty, we are led to inquire how Berthier
really did perform it in his day, and whether mistakes
and carelessness in the transmission of Napoleon's
orders began with the campaign of Waterloo. This is
a matter on which the most clear and direct evidence

Vie de
Napoléon,
i. 346.
is happily at hand.   Jomini has recorded the fact that,
in 1807, the capture of a single messenger delayed
the arrival of Bernadotte's corps two days, and left
him out of the hard-fought battle of Eylau.   The
same author, writing in a spirit favourable to Napoleon, but not desirous to screen Berthier's faults,
Ibid. ii. 70. shows that in 1809, at the passage of the Danube
before Wagram, Davoust's and Oudinot's orders sent
their corps to the wrong bridges, and obliged their
troops to cross each other's line of march after the
passage was made.   Nor are these solitary instances.
This historian, who served on the French staff in both
Ibid. ii.
294. campaigns, was present in a similar capacity at Baut-
zen in 1813.   Here he bears express testimony to the
fact, that the incompleteness of that great victory was
directly due to the insufficiency of the orders received
from Napoleon by Marshal Ney, to whom he himself
was chief of staff.   In all these cases he speaks not
merely with the authority of a great military critic, but
that of an observant eyewitness.   As a biographer he
is disposed to rate Napoleon's genius at its highest, as
the form and execution of his work alike imply : yet
on three critical occasions he shows the staff system of
the Grand Army to have broken down from want of
care in the controlling hand.

  After this we may well be prepared for the severe
picture of the system in its nicer details, which the
faithful hand of the Duc de Fezensac has painted.
This author, who served constantly on the French staff
from 1806 to 1813, and watched its working in times

of disaster as well as through a long period of success, has thus described its deficiencies :—

'Long journeys on duty were made in carriages Fez.p.118. charged at the post rate ; but some officers put the money in their pockets, and obtained horses by requisition.   This was a bad plan in every view, for, apart from the dishonesty, they were ill served and lost valuable time.   As for messages taken on horseback, I have already said that no person took the pains to inquire if we had a horse that could walk, even when it was necessary to go at a gallop ; or if we knew the country, or had a map.   The order must be executed without waiting for the means, as I shall show in some special instances.   This habit of attempting everything with the most feeble instruments, this wish to overlook impossibilities, this unbounded assurance of success, which at first helped to win us advantages, in the end became our destruction.'

Again, speaking of himself carrying most impor- Ibid. p. 145. tant orders to Ney on the morning of the day of Eylau : 'My horse was already worn out when I received the orders at 8 a.m., and with difficulty could I, being fortunately in funds, buy a restive animal to carry me.   I knew nothing of the roads, and had no guide.   To ask for an escort would have been of no more use than to ask for a horse.   An officer always had an excellent horse, knew the country, was never taken, met no accident, and got rapidly to his destination ; and of all this there was so little doubt, *that often a second message was thought unnecessary.*'

After such evidence we may well afford to dismiss
the theory of Thiers, that any personal incompetence
of Soult in the management of the staff formed an
element in the disaster of 1815. But we have a
special reason for rejecting his statement in this matter.
Telling us, as he does repeatedly, that his assertions
are based on careful comparison of official reports
with the narratives of eyewitnesses, Thiers rarely
quotes the original authority which he prefers to
follow. How can we accept any assertion as to Napoleon's staff service made by a writer who does not

Thi. vii.
372.

scruple to declare, that several (' plusieurs ') officers
were dispatched *the night before the battle* of Eylau to
call in Davoust and Ney, when, from the Duc de
Fezensac's evidence—given after he read this assertion
—we find that the only orders ever dispatched to Ney
to this effect were in the single dispatch carried *on the
morning of the battle* by himself ? But we shall find,
as we follow our subject onwards, other misstatements
not less gross made by Thiers, even in details on the
French side, than that here exposed.

Ante, p.71.

After the admission by this historian of the truth
as to the desertion of Bourmont, it might seem super-

Mém. ix.
162.
Gourg.
p. 34.

fluous to notice further the erroneous assertions of the
St. Helena narratives, that that traitor went over ' on
the evening of,' or ' during the day of,' the 14th. But
these narratives, though ill agreeing with each other,
have misled a host of writers on this and other points,
and the amount of credit to be accorded to their
assertions *where Napoleon's own character* is concerned,

is one of the most important branches of our subject. It is necessary, therefore, to point out plainly (what seems to have usually escaped notice), that the flight Doc. 141. being assigned to the 14th is a pure afterthought, originated at St. Helena. The bulletin of the evening of the 15th proves this sufficiently. After an explicit mention that Gérard had reported the desertion follows a line which states that he had *that evening arrived* at Châtelet. This is not the only instance in which Napoleon writing history is actually less accurate than Napoleon writing bulletins! A valuable Hooper, p. 68. note on the subject of the evidence of Sir F. Head as to Bourmont's arrival at Charleroi is given by Hooper ; but that author seems to have overlooked the narrative of Colonel Janin before referred to, or he Ibid. Ante, p.70. would hardly have assumed, as he has done too easily, that Soult ' neglected to send ' Vandamme the order of march.

The particulars we have given of the movement concerted by the Allies for the very case of invasion that happened sufficiently show that the importance of the Charleroi, Quatre Bras, and Sombreffe triangle was fully recognised by them beforehand. It has been generally said (Siborne, for instance, explicitly states), Sib. i. 39. that the two northern angles of this were designed for the concentration of the two Allied armies respectively. Distinct authority for the assertion has never been given ; and we must believe that Müffling, an officer of special experience, who was in the confidence of both Marshals, and perfectly conversant with the details

See ante
p. 73.

discussed in their Tirlemont meeting, is better informed, when he fixes the intended concentration some miles further to the south and nearer Charleroi. This view is supported by the fact, that the position he assigns would have brought the armies within better supporting distance than if placed (as Siborne and others would have it), the one at Ligny, the other at Quatre Bras, with a space of several miles between their inner wings.

Zieten's deliberate retreat on Fleurus and Ligny, the masterly way in which he collected his scattered corps during the movement, and the fine front with which he held back Vandamme before the former place, have long attracted the admiration of military critics. Colonel Hamley, in his valuable work on War, has taken it for his special example of the conduct of such an operation, and to that work we may, therefore, well refer for the details. At the same time it must not be forgotten, that there seems no sufficient reason for the omission as to the Sambre bridges already noted ; still less for not communicating instantly to the Prince of Orange, and General Dornberg at Mons, the certain withdrawal of the Prussian parties on their left. Had a proper connection been maintained between Zieten's videttes, which filled the line from Thuin to Bonne Espérance, and those of Dornberg westward of that place, the latter general should have been earlier warned* of the advance in

Opera-
tions of
War, p.
128 et seq.

Ante, p.82.

Pr. Off.
p. 12.

---

* It has been shown from General Rebecque's journal (published in 'Militair Wochenblatt,' of Berlin, 1846), that Steinmetz, the

force on Marchiennes, and might have well anticipated the missive of Zieten to Brussels, the slowness of which cannot, in any case, be excused. It must be added that the Prussian loss (usually given as 1,200 for the day) is understated. Like that for the 16th it fails to include the ' missing.' But in the official narrative we find that one battalion was ' pierced by cavalry, sabred or taken,' and another, ' reached by the enemy, lost two-thirds its numbers.' The loss for the two days, of 15th and 16th, reduced officially to 12,078, is given in distinct terms in Müffling's early narrative as 20,900. The difference is of course in ' missing ' men, partly prisoners ; and it will be reasonable to add to Zieten's admitted 1,200 enough of these to make his loss quite as great as the 2,000 assigned him by French historians. Even with this, and the other drawbacks mentioned, the retreat, so ably conducted before the tremendous force which Napoleon pressed on him, must always redound to the credit of the Prussian general.

We pass to one of the most serious controversies bound up with the history of the campaign. This concerns the verbal orders of Napoleon to Ney on the afternoon of the 15th, and the spirit in which they were carried out. It hardly admits of doubt, that had Ney briskly attacked Prince Bernard, he might

Margin notes:
Pr. Off. p. 16.
Ibid. p. 47.
Ibid. p. 12.
Ibid. p. 15.
Ibid. p. 47.
Müff. Hist. p. 10.

---

nearest to the English of the Prussian brigadiers, did send a message of alarm at 8 a.m. to his Belgian neighbour, Van Merlen. Admitting this to be true, the late arrival of the intelligence at Brussels seems to prove, that the step taken was insufficient, or not early enough, or both.

have seized the position of Quatre Bras at a stroke ;
for though his infantry little exceeded the Nassauers
Cha. p. 90.
Thi. xx.46. in number, they were as veterans superior in morale,
and were supported by a fine force of cavalry of not
less than 4,000 sabres, to which Bernard had none to
oppose.   Now, to take up ground anywhere near the
Prussians, Wellington's troops must pass through
Quatre Bras ; and that place was, in such case, the
natural point marked for his Reserve to join the 1st
and 2nd Corps by the most direct roads available.   In
short, we know now that it was of more actual importance for some of his troops to hold it than he had
recognised that day, before aware of the full progress
of the French ; and it becomes important to know
whose is the responsibility for Ney's resolve to halt at
Frasnes.

Whole works have been devoted to the subject of
this and two other alleged faults of the Marshal.   But
Thi. xx.47,
et seq.note. we may be spared a library of controversy, for Thiers
has devoted a special note to the matter we are considering, and has pleaded the cause of the Emperor
against Ney with a dexterity and vigour such as no
meaner advocate can match, and which leaves further
argument on that side hopeless.   When we analyse all
he has said, however, the exact result produced is the
following :—There were four persons present at the
colloquy near Charleroi, viz. Napoleon, Ney, Soult, and
Colonel Heymès, the only staff officer who arrived
with the Marshal when he reported himself.   Ney
died before the controversy arose.   Soult contradicted

to others a declaration of his to Ney's son, the late Duc d'Elchingen, that his father had no order to push on to Quatre Bras, and Soult's evidence is, therefore, untrustworthy. Heymès, it is true, declares the order was a merely general one, ' Allez et poussez l'ennemi ; ' but Heymès' evidence is to be rejected, *because he wrote his work ' expressly to prove* that the Marshal committed not a single mistake.' There remains only Napoleon, and Napoleon is to be credited, because, in his first St. Helena version, he gives such precise details of the conversation that ' it is impossible to suppose that he has falsified the truth.' Now, without trying Napoleon's evidence by the severe test the historian has applied to that of Heymès (which we need hardly point out would vitiate it hopelessly), we will put it to the proof of Thiers' own opinion of Napoleon's veracity on a like occasion at a former time. Two years before Waterloo, Vandamme's corps had been destroyed at Kulm by a rash adventure into the rear of the Allied army. Vandamme himself was for some days reported dead, though really taken ; and how his master occupied the interval, let Thiers' own significant expressions tell :

' When Vandamme's secretary reappeared, Napoleon had the general's papers seized, that he might extract from it all his military correspondence, and thus remove all proof of the orders which this unfortunate officer had received from him. Napoleon had even the weakness to deny that he had given him orders to march upon Tœplitz, and wrote to all the

[margin notes:] Mém. ix. 251.

Gourg. p. 40, n.

Thi. xvi. 400.

commanders of corps, that this general, having received instructions to halt upon the heights of Kulm,
had been carried away by a too ardent spirit, and
had been destroyed through an excess of zeal. The
authentic narrative which we have given of the facts
proves the falsity of these assertions.'

Thi. xx.
49 n. Yet this is the same Napoleon of whom Thiers
would have us believe that, three years later, in com-
posing the Gourgaud narrative, ' he of all contempo-
raries falsified the least, and counted too securely on
his own glory to found it on the depreciation of his
lieutenants.' Surely an historian pays heavily for a
theory when it leads him into such a contradiction of
himself as this! In truth, if Ney spoke not, his
action confirms the story of Heymès, and that told
Ney's son by Soult, and of itself fully contradicts the
Napoleon version.

' But,' continues Thiers, after discussing the evidence, ' there is another sort of proof superior, in my
view, to all human witness ; that is, the probability.'
Let us look at the matter in this light also. Did Napoleon, in advancing from Charleroi on the two sides
of the Fleurus triangle, intend to occupy both Quatre
Bras and Sombreffe, if possible ; or, if that were not
so, to seize one and not the other. This is a question
of probabilities which General Jomini, a critic of the
highest order, and writing in a sense very favourable
Jomini,
p. 153. to Napoleon, has specially discussed. Jomini decides
for the veracity of the ' Gourgaud ' version, but upon
grounds which afford a peculiarly valuable instance

of the danger of theorising before facts are established. The positive order to advance to Quatre Bras must have been given, he thinks, ' in the same manner as to Grouchy ' [then with the advance on the other road], ' whom he ordered to push to Sombreffe, if that were possible ; ' for, as the writer has previously remarked, ' the most simple glance at the map indicates sufficiently that it was necessary to occupy both.' Thiers, however, has taken pains to prove, from Napoleon's own words, that the Emperor's deliberate design was not to occupy Sombreffe that night. To do this was, in his own words,* at least in one of his versions, just that which ' he took special care to avoid.' Theoretically, therefore, if Jomini be an authority, Quatre Bras ought not to have been occupied that evening, *for Sombreffe was not to be and was not so* ; and for Ney to push his advance-guard on, without any co-operating movement, would have been to place it haphazard just between an uncertain force of the English army and a large body, certainly present, of the Prussians. ' If he had done thus,' remarks Quinet, whose admirable chapter on this head should be studied, ' he would have been charged with temerity, and not without cause. Thus strategic proof is joined to the evidence of documents.'

Jomini, p. 154, *n.* Ibid. p. 153.

Thi. xx. 43.

Mém. viii. 196.

Quin. 92, *et seq.*

Ibid. p. 103.

---

* The version that Thiers here uses is from a reply by Napoleon to the severe strictures on his strategy published in General Rogniat's ' Considérations sur l'Art de la Guerre.' But it must be observed that this conflicts with the ex-Emperor's other accounts in the Gourgaud and Mémoires (tom. ix.) histories; a discrepancy which will not surprise anyone who studies critically the St. Helena writings.

If neither of these suffice, we may fitly close our examination of this question with an extract from Napoleon's own latest version, which, if it were trustworthy, would decide the matter of itself against the writer. ' Ney received the order, *in the night*, to move on the 16th at break of day to beyond Quatre Bras, and take up a good position across the Brussels road, holding those to Nivelles and Namur ; ' to do, in fact, what in other places Napoleon has said he was ordered to do the evening before ; and this is written without a word of reference as to any failure of the Marshal's to carry out his first instructions !

Mém. ix. 79.

Passing to the operations of the other side, it has been shown that Bernard deserves full credit for the original occupation of Quatre Bras—credit to be shared by Rebecque and Perponcher for their approval of it. That the young Prince only that day for the first time had charge of a brigade, adds considerably to the merit of his conduct. It is a singular proof of the gross carelessness of Thiers in details relating to the Allies, that in his account of the day's affairs, he makes Bernard march with his 4,000 men *from Nivelles* to Quatre Bras on his own account. Thus, though he gives the Prince credit for the occupation, he robs Perponcher to do so ; for he would have the former effect it by leaving without orders the station which was the headquarters of his own division general there present, ' under the simple inspiration of common sense,' a remarkable military achievement certainly for any brigadier to accomplish.

Thi. xx.46.

Loben S. p. 130.

It would be well if certain other misstatements of this historian, as to the movements of Perponcher's men, which we must presently notice, were as little harmless as this.

Of the celebrated misunderstanding of Bülow's orders by that general it is necessary to say but little, the facts being fully admitted as we have given them. It remains a warning for future generals in the place of Gneisenau, to put the first orders for a sudden campaign into some form not to be mistaken for an ordinary movement.   A little special care in explaining to Bülow the state of the case would have been derogatory to no one writing to a general who had held a chief command himself with honour, and would have spared the error that cost the Prussians dear in the loss of 30,000 men at the hour of need.

Ante, p. 77.

Wellington's inaction during the 15th can hardly escape notice in the most cursory view of the strategy of this campaign.   As might be expected, it has found severe critics and warm defenders.   Of the latter we may specially notice Hooper, who insists that Wellington's first orders contained all that was needful to be done upon the information received in the afternoon. But this defence has the ground cut from under it by the Duke's own account of the campaign, from which we have quoted in our narrative.   It is true that his memory when he wrote that account was no longer exact ; but in saying, that upon the first news received (at 3 p.m.) the whole army was forthwith ordered to its left, Wellington clearly gives his own impression,

Hooper, p. 79, &c.

See ante, p. 78, n.

in 1842, of what he ought to have done in 1815. It is no answer to criticism to say with Hooper, that he, ' never precipitate or nervous, contented himself with issuing orders about 5 p.m. for the assembly of each division.' This is a statement of the fact, but no justi-fication of it. This same author has taken much pains to defend Wellington from the censure of Charras, and has succeeded in discovering one blunder (relative to the time that the alarm reached the Duke) made by the latter from his imperfect knowledge of English. But he himself is hypercritical when he objects further to Charras's next remark, that ' thus the few troops on the Brussels road were to be removed in the very case of an attack on the right of the Prussian and left of the English army.' These particular words are used in the order to Alten's British division, and not in that to Perponcher's, it is true ; but the fact is, that the command to the latter to collect his Dutch-Belgians at Nivelles, seven miles off the Brussels road, was making the very mistake of which Charras com-plains. Indeed, Hooper in the same paragraph admits that Perponcher took upon himself to disobey, and deserves credit for it ; an admission which settles the question of fact as to the propriety of the order he received.

In the same paragraph Hooper asserts, and no doubt justly, that Wellington would have done what Perponcher did had he been at Nivelles or Braine. This brings us at once to the real issue. Was Wel-lington in his right place at Brussels on the 15th, and

Hooper, p. 81.

Ibid. p. 82.

Cha. p. 10.

Hooper, p. 84.

especially in the evening, after his news from the front ? Clausewitz says distinctly that Wellington's headquarters should have been moved to Nivelles on its being known that the French were gathering. This, and the criticisms of other Continental critics, may by some be thought of little importance ; but it cannot be unimportant to observe that Müffling, the most friendly to the Duke of this class, agrees exactly with his countryman on this head. While denying that the English cantonments were too dispersed, he adds, ' that if the Duke had left Brussels on the 14th, at nine o'clock on the 15th he would have heard the cannonade. In that case Napoleon would have fallen into the Caudine Forks on the 16th.' Claus. p. 46. Mü. Mém. p. 233.

Such are not the views that are popular with the mass of English writers, but they are substantially the same as those of two recent critics of our own nation, each of whom thoroughly admires Wellington, and has done something towards making his real greatness better known. Colonel Hamley has written, of the evening's stay at Brussels : ' We must believe that the Duke was throwing away golden minutes. By riding himself towards Charleroi at the first alarm, he would have seen for himself that this was no feint, and by next morning assembled troops there sufficient to check Ney and aid Blücher.' Kennedy goes further, and declares that, before the 15th, both armies should have been cantoned much nearer Brussels, so that, on the French being known to be in motion, Blücher's might have at once assembled near Genappe, and Welling-ton's Ca-reer, p. 77. Kenn. p. 171, 172.

H

Wellington's at Hal, or in some similar positions, suitable for mutual support.

Summary.

To sum up the facts of the 15th as they occurred. It has been shown that Napoleon failed, owing to incomplete arrangements on his own side, to bring his whole army over the Sambre as he had intended, yet had nearly 100,000 men at night on the north bank; that the Allied generals had considered beforehand the very case that was about to happen, and determined on certain positions to be occupied in the Fleurus triangle; that Blücher had one of his corps on the intended ground, and two more near, but had failed to bring his fourth within available distance; that Wellington moved not a man to meet the enemy, and ordered a concentration which would have left Ney at liberty to push on within fourteen miles of Brussels; and that Napoleon had actually in his possession, on this first day of the campaign, the whole of the ground on which the English were to have met him, with his advanced guard holding a portion of that originally marked out for Blücher. Up to this point it can surely be asserted that the balance of strategy was on his side.

LECTURE IV.

EVENTS OF THE 16TH.—COMMENTS.—SUMMARY.

THE advantage gained by Napoleon's early movement of the 15th being so clear, it is the more difficult to explain why so little was done on the morning of the next day to carry out the conception of a surprise. Ney spent many hours of the night with the Emperor, Cha.p.114.
Thi.xx.52. and only left him at about 2 a.m., without any positive orders for the morning's movements. At about 6 a.m. Cha.p.117.
Thi.xx.61. a report from Grouchy told Napoleon, then some time risen, that the Prussian army (in fact, the troops of Pirch joining those of Zieten) was deploying before Fleurus. Yet it was not until 8 a.m. (as Charras has Cha.p.117. shown by overwhelming testimony) that the dispositions were conceived upon which the day's movements were to be carried out, and the corresponding orders issued. The mass of the army was now to be formed into two wings, each to act on one side of the Fleurus triangle. Grouchy took command of Gérard's and See Orig.
Order.
Mém. ix.
333, &c. Vandamme's troops, and three of the four corps of reserve cavalry. With these he was 'to march on Sombreffe, and take up a position there.' As soon as he had possession of Sombreffe, he was further enjoined 'to send an advanced guard to Gembloux [a large village five miles to the N.E.] and reconnoitre all the roads from Sombreffe, especially that to Namur, establishing also communications with Marshal Ney.'

See ante, p. 75.

To the latter's command, as already detailed, the remaining corps of reserve cavalry (Kellermann's) was added. He was ordered, in a letter from Soult, to put his troops in motion for Trois Bras [Quatre Bras], take up a position there, and reconnoitre the Brussels and Nivelles roads. 'If it should not be inconvenient,' he was further to push a division and some cavalry on to Genappe, and to post another division at Marbais,* placing the cavalry of the Guard near to these two. 'The Emperor,' it was added, 'is going to Sombreffe.' Grouchy's orders were noted for Ney's information.

See Orig. Sib. i. 449, quoted by Cha.p.116.

As above, Sib.orCha.

Simultaneously with this letter, Napoleon dictated a separate one to Ney, repeating its tenor in a more detailed form. 'He is pushing on Grouchy; he will be himself at Fleurus before noon; will attack the enemy, if met with, and clear the road to Gembloux.' 'There, at 3 p.m., or perhaps in the evening,' he adds, 'I will decide on my course according to what may occur. My intention is, immediately after I have decided, that you be ready to march on Brussels. I will support you with the Guard, and I should wish to arrive at Brussels to-morrow morning.' Details are added of the proposed march, of the temporary position

---

* Marbais is a village about a quarter of a mile to the north of the Namur-Nivelles road, at exactly halfway from Sombreffe to Quatre Bras.

to be taken up at and beyond Quatre Bras, and of the Emperor's new division of the army into two grand wings under Grouchy and Ney, with a reserve (of the troops not attached to these Marshals) under himself. Ney was particularly directed to take care of the Guard cavalry, and rather to employ that of the line, should there be any skirmish (*quelque échauffourée*) with the English. A strikingly similar letter of instructions to Grouchy, first published by Charras in the fourth edition of his work, and written certainly after 8 a.m., declares ' the Prussians are not able to bring more than 40,000 men against us,' and speaks of getting to Brussels the next day without a serious action. So little did the Emperor foresee the promptitude of Blücher, or conceive it necessary to hasten his own movements. *Cha. Ed. 1863, p. 134.*

Gérard, lying not quite four miles from Charleroi, has stated that he did not receive his orders until half-past 9 ; and the other generals on that side had theirs, no doubt, at corresponding hours. On the left, or Brussels road, Count Flahault, with the Emperor's order to Ney, passed Gosselies at about 10, communicating to Reille its contents (who reported his passage by at a quarter after 10), and reaching Ney, who waited at Frasnes, soon after—' towards 11 o'clock,' according to the testimony of Colonel Heymès. The Marshal had been reconnoitring the position of Quatre Bras, now occupied by a whole Dutch-Belgian division under the Prince of Orange and his Staff, and had sent an officer off to report to the Emperor that *Cha.p.117, after Gérard's ' Documents.' See his letter to Ney, Sib. i. 451.* *Cha.p.181. Report lost, but known by reply.*

the enemy showed masses of men there. The reply to this was a third dispatch, sent after the official one of Soult (which again was a little later than that borne by Flahault, as the words of each prove), desiring Ney 'to unite the corps of Reille and D'Erlon with that of Kellermann (the reserve cavalry corps allotted the Marshal), and with these to beat and destroy any enemy who should oppose him.' 'Blücher cannot have pushed troops towards Quatre Bras, for he was only yesterday at Namur. You have only, therefore, to deal with what comes from Brussels.'

See Orig. Mém. ix. 337.

Sib. i. 451.

On the receipt of the Emperor's own letter, Ney sent his corresponding instructions forthwith to Reille, who was to move one division on Genappe, another to support it, and the two remaining ones to Quatre Bras. D'Erlon was to move three divisions to Frasnes, and send one to Marbais; Kellermann and the Guard cavalry to stay at Frasnes for the present. It will be remembered, however, that one of Reille's four divisions had been kept away from him the night before, and left near Vandamme, at the village of Wangenies. The general who led it (Girard) had been watching the Prussians form on the Ligny heights, and made report by an officer accordingly to Reille ; and Reille, receiving this intelligence, did not choose to advance upon Flahault's instance, but sent Girard's officer forward to Ney, to communicate the news, and request instructions—a natural caution, considering that, in moving on Frasnes, he would have the Prussians within three and a half miles of the right of

See Reille's Letter. Sib. i. 452.

his columns. On Ney's orders arriving, or on a change
of mind as to this supposed danger, he moved forwards
about 11 a.m. His troops, however, had six long See
Reille's
Notice
miles of road to make before Ney was reached. Foy's Notice
division, which led, could not attain Frasnes before Histo-
rique,
1 at the earliest, and had then to form up and quoted by
Cha.p.151.
deploy. At about 2 o'clock, the French advanced
from Frasnes in force, according to the report of the
Prince of Orange, a personal eye-witness, in command Doc. 86.
on one side, and the ' Notice ' of Reille on the other, Cha.p.155.
and rather earlier by the statements of Heymès, Mém. ix.
256.
speaking for Ney, and of the Dutch officers of Perponcher's division, who have left several accounts, all
placing the real attack between 1 and 2 o'clock. Loben S.
p. 190.
Then began, as far as the French were concerned, the
battle of Quatre Bras. By half-past 3 the Netherland
troops opposed to Ney were rudely pressed back to
the cross roads, according to the admission of their
own historian, though they still held the little wood Ibid 195.
close to them. It is important to be particular here
as to time, as one of the chief of the figments which
have passed into Waterloo history concerns this point
of the campaign.

We left Napoleon sending out his orders between
8 and 9 a.m. The early part of the morning had not
been wholly wasted, since those of the French left on
the south bank of the Sambre completed their passages at Charleroi and Châtelet, and joined the main
body. Vandamme meanwhile, and the rest of the
troops which had halted before Fleurus the night

before, now passed beyond that place, abandoned by
the Prussians, and took ground in the open plain
beyond, in full sight of the hill of Ligny. Napoleon
did not join them until near noon. Lobau's corps
was left for a time at the junction of the two roads
close to Charleroi, but the Guard followed the Emperor and formed in front of the position now plainly
seen to be occupied in great force by the enemy.
Napoleon had with him there the wing assigned to
Grouchy, with the infantry of the Guard, and that
division detached from Reille which had kept on Vandamme's left at night at Wangenies (by Thiers twice
called erroneously Wagnelée), and still remained detached from its own corps. His original force, omitting non-combatants of the train, was thus distributed
at noon :—

With Ney 45,000
  ,, Napoleon 64,000
  ,, Lobau (to support either) . 10,000
In rear 5,000
                                        ——————
                                     124,000

At 2 p.m. the Emperor had made his resolve fully.
A short letter informed Ney that ' Grouchy was to
attack at half-past 2, a body (*un corps*) of the enemy
posted between Sombreffe and Bry.* Ney was also to
attack sharply what was before him, and after driving
it off vigorously, to wheel and aid in enveloping this

---

    * A village 1¼ mile N.W. of Ligny, and on the flat part of the
plateau, the latter place being on the slope in the centre of the
position, and St. Amand on the Prussian right.

Cha.p.118.
Thi.xx.74.

Thi. xx.
54, 72.

Cha.p.125.
Thi.xx.63.

See Orig.
Sib. i. 453.
Cha.p.122.

" corps." If the latter were first pierced, then the
Emperor would manœuvre in the Marshal's direction.'
At about 3 p.m., somewhat later than the appointed
time, the battle of Ligny was begun by Grouchy's
troops, it being then about an hour after Ney advanced from Frasnes.

Gourg.
p. 48, 'à
3 heures.'
Pr. Off. 28.
' vers 3
heures.'

To pass to the Allies. Of the Prussians it is sufficient to say that, by the time Napoleon's morning
orders were issued, not Pirch only but Thielemann had
reached the destined battle-ground, and Blucher stood
awaiting the shock of what he thought the whole army
of the enemy with 85,000 men, Bülow being too far
off to be of any service that day. Turning to Quatre
Bras, where Bernard's brigade was alone the night
before, we find that of Bylandt (the other half of
Perponcher's division) beginning to arrive by separate
battalions as early as 4 a.m. (' towards morning '
is the expression of Bernard himself, in a letter
of the 19th June), and all on the ground at 9, save
a single battalion, which did not quit Nivelles until
Alten's troops appeared, and was not up before 3.
Perponcher, who had arranged this movement, and
left General Bylandt to start the brigade, came up
himself at 3 a.m. to take command ; but at 6 a.m. the
Prince of Orange rode in from Braine for the same
purpose. The former had begun, and the latter now
continued a light infantry advance, before which the
French posts fell back towards Frasnes, near which
the skirmish ceased. About 11 Wellington arrived
from Brussels with his staff, and after reconnoitring

See his Re-
port, Doc.
89.

Loben S.
p. 185.

Doc. 85.

Loben S.
p. 193.
Ibid. p.183.

Loben S.
p. 185.

Ibid. 187.
Sib. i. 92.

the enemy, and finding them motionless, rode on to meet Blücher at Bry, on the Ligny heights, where their plans for the day were settled. An interesting account of the interview is to be read in the work of Müffling. None of those present thought seriously of the force before Quatre Bras : all believed Napoleon's army, regarded as one body, was before Ligny ; and the question discussed was chiefly whether the movement of Wellington's troops should be to the rear of the Prussians to act as a reserve, or to their right to outflank the advancing French. Gneisenau was so strongly in favour of the former, that the Duke and Müffling (who both inclined to the other proposal) yielded their views to his, and left again for Quatre Bras, the Duke saying to Gneisenau, ' Well, I will come, *provided I am not attacked myself.*' On returning to the Prince of Orange, they found the troops with him already sorely pressed, and were only relieved from the imminent danger of losing the crossroads by the arrival of Picton, who came up from Waterloo at about 3 p.m.,* Van Merlen's brigade of Dutch-Belgian cavalry arriving from Nivelles almost simultaneously. These aided to hold the position until more reinforcements supported them in turn, and

Mü. Mem. p. 233, &c.

Loben S. 197.
Sib. i. 105.

* The Duke's official report (Gurw. Disp.) would make this half-past 2. But this is corrected by a note in the Sup. Disp. (x. 525), which fixes the Duke's own return from Ligny—universally admitted to be *previous* to Picton's arrival—to be 'about 3.' Loben Sels, from the accounts of the Dutch-Belgians (p. 194), makes it 'between 3 and 4.' The Prince of Orange reported Van Merlen—who is known from all accounts to have been hardly later—not up till 4.

Wellington began to feel his forces superior to those
of his antagonist. Ney received in due course the
2 o'clock order of Napoleon, but was too hotly engaged
already to do anything towards executing a wheel
upon Marbais beyond pressing his attacks on the
defenders of Quatre Bras. This order arrived some-
where between half-past 3 and 5, and produced no
special change in the order of events. The fight
grew harder for the French as the afternoon wore
on, and brought no news of the corps of D'Erlon,
whose 20,000 men should have been ere now arriving
at Frasnes. At 6 came the fifth and last order that
day received, written by Napoleon from before Ligny
soon after the battle there had begun, and dated at
a quarter after three. The cool ease which marks
the tone of those preceding had now disappeared,
for Napoleon had felt his enemy's strength. The
delusions about the occupying Sombreffe and pushing
beyond it are no longer referred to. ' At this moment
the battle is going on hotly [*est très prononcé*]. His
Majesty desires me to tell you, that you are to
manœuvre immediately in such a manner as to en-
velope the right of the enemy, and fall upon his rear.
The fate of France is in your hands.' Hereon Ney in
his turn called on Kellermann, and another desperate
attack was made, to be repulsed by the arrival of the
English Guards. Wellington had now over 30,000
men upon the ground, and before dark in his turn
took the offensive and drove back the exhausted foe
to the position at Frasnes, which he had that morning

See ante,
pp. 104,
105.

Thi. xx.
105.
Cha.p.162.

For detail,
Sib. i. 153.

Thi. xx.
126.
Cha.p.168. held. As Ney paused here at nightfall, the missing corps of D'Erlon began to come in from a strange march made intermediately between the two battles, summoned back in fact from an ill-judged attempt to join Napoleon by the urgent instance of his over-matched lieutenant, but arriving far too late to save him his defeat.

This movement of the 1st Corps seriously affected the completeness of Napoleon's success, if we are to accept his original account, which tells graphically how this occurred.   The desperate fight at Ligny had been raging for two or three hours along the Prussian front, and more particularly on the right, where Vandamme, aided by Girard's division, attacked again and again the St. Amand hamlets.   Napoleon himself, in accord-ance with his favourite tactics, was ranging the Guard in order for the purpose of giving the final stroke, which he had reserved until the whole of his enemy's troops were entangled in indecisive combats, when a Gourg.
p. 49. dense column was seen by Vandamme ' a league to his own left, heading apparently from Fleurus, and turning the flank of the French line.'   The Emperor, on report of this appearance, checked his Guard and prepared to receive the supposed dangerous intruder. Ibid. p. 50. It was half-past six before word came that it was no Prussian or English force, but the corps of D'Erlon which had caused the alarm ; and the new change of position necessary to prepare the reserve once more for the attack on Ligny (where Blücher's line was to be attempted) lost Napoleon another half-hour.   The

attack was made successfully, without employing
D'Erlon or even Lobau, who had been ordered up
from his halting-ground near Charleroi, but the result Gourg.
p. 51.
came too late.   As is well known, the Prussian centre See also
Pr. Off.
was pierced and their position carried with the loss of pp. 45–47.
twenty-one guns ; Blücher himself was much hurt in Mil.Woch.
for 1869,
a charge made to check the enemy's advance, shortly p. 708.
after he had dispatched Major Winterfeldt, one of his
aides-de-camp, to acquaint Wellington that he was
forced to retreat.

But darkness prevented the French from profiting
by their advantage, and only a few of their cavalry
reached the Namur road that night.   Three battalions Ibid. 47.
of Prussians passed it in the village of Bry, close to
the French ; for it was 10 p.m. and too dark to move,
before Gneisenau's orders (he having taken command
in Blücher's absence) reached the scattered corps,
directing a general retreat due northward on Wavre.
As to D'Erlon (who had received on his way across an
imperative message from Ney by his own chief of staff,
ordering his return to the Quatre Bras side), after a Thi. xx.
124.
halt that showed some indecision, he left one of his Cha.p.174.
divisions to support Napoleon's battle, and with the
rest moved on Frasnes, where he arrived, as has been
mentioned, too late to be of any use that day.   So
closed the bloody contests of the 16th.   Wellington,
holding Quatre Bras, rode off to sleep at Genappe, Mü. Mem.
p. 239.
ignorant of the extent of his ally's defeat, while Ney Supp.
was still more ill-informed of the Emperor's success. Disp.
x. 526.
In our next chapter we shall note the positions of Mém. ix.
340.

such of the Allied troops as failed to appear at the
scenes of action ; it is sufficient here to point out that
these amounted on the Prussian side to 30,000 men,
on the English to 62,000, even after allowing for the
troops left purposely in garrison.

Comments.

'The chief reproach as to the [French] operations
of the 16th is the time lost on the morning of that

Thi. xx.
127.

day.' Such are the words in which Thiers puts the
charge he would disprove ; and in order to see how
far Napoleon is responsible for the delay, we shall follow as before that masterly advocate, sure that if he
cannot succeed in exculpating the Emperor, no other

Thi. xx.
128.

will be able to do so. 'Three hours,' he proceeds,
'were needed (so many of the troops being to the
south of the Sambre) before the various corps could
be placed ready to advance into any required line of
battle. Napoleon was unwilling to act without good
information, and waited for Grouchy's report of what
the Prussians were doing. This did not reach Charleroi till after 7 a.m., and the orders were all dispatched before 9.' Such is in brief his explanation of
the first part of the delay, by which *not three but
seven* hours were lost in truth, since daylight broke
at 3 a.m., and the troops made no movement until
10 o'clock, except so far as concerns the passage of
the river. 'After the instructions were sent out,'
the defence continues, 'Napoleon stayed still at Charleroi, gathering information and issuing orders, for

it was necessary to give time for the troops to march on Fleurus. Besides, the day was at least seventeen hours long, and the battle might as well be fought in the afternoon as the morning. Arrived at Ligny before noon, the Emperor did not, like his generals, hesitate ; but he was compelled to wait for part of Gérard's troops not up. Thus he was kept until two, Thi. xx. and then waited for Ney to get the start of him, and 129. take the Prussians in rear. The false alarm raised by Vandamme ' [*i.e.* about D'Erlon's corps] ' accounts Ibid. 130. for the loss of an hour and a half in the middle of the battle, and its late and unsatisfactory close. No, Napoleon personally must not be charged with inac- Ibid. 127. tivity, although this reproach is perfectly well founded as concerns all that went on on the side of Quatre Bras.' Such is the substance of a most ingenious and elaborate misstatement of the case, the shortest reply to which is to admit first, for argument's sake, the supposed facts, and to reason upon them as accepted. Whose fault is it, then, this well-founded reproach as to Quatre Bras ? Did Napoleon, having learnt from Ney (as Thiers admits) at supper on the Ibid. 47. 15th the non-occupation of that place during the evening, order any early movement towards it ? Did he direct that at daylight D'Erlon should close up his long column on Reille's rear at Gosselies, and be ready for the marching order forward ? Were there any signs of pressure or hurry in Ney's morning instructions, or any notion then of a great pitched battle which that Marshal was by a flank movement

to win for his master ?　We are enabled to answer
all these questions in the direct negative from
See Orig.
Mém. ix.
335.
Napoleon's own authority.　The only letter from the
latter to Ney written before the five orders already
mentioned was merely a formal one, assigning Kellermann's cavalry to the Marshal, and inquiring if
D'Erlon had completed his movement [of the day
before], and ' what are the exact positions of his
corps and Reille's ? '　Not a word of any urgency,
or of preparing to advance by closing D'Erlon's
divisions on to the chaussée at Gosselies.　As to the
8 o'clock instructions themselves, we need not look
for them in the appendix to the ' Mémoires ; ' nor
need we pause in order to contradict the shameless
Mém. ix.
78.
Cha.p.178.
falsehood there told, that ' Ney was ordered in the
night to advance on Quatre Bras at daylight.'　Charras
has exposed this with remorseless severity ; nor does
Thiers attempt to use any such pretended verbal
order, the plainest proof that it is a hopeless fabrica-
tion.　Indeed, we may be quite sure it would not
See ante,
p. 100.
have been published had the ex-Emperor known that
his real orders of the morning would have seen the
light, as they did nearly twenty years later, thanks
to the interest of Ney's son in the matter.　It is only
necessary to look back to these to see clearly what
Napoleon had in his mind on the morning of the
day of which we are speaking.

It is necessary here to make a distinct protest,
once for all, against the inaccurate mode of reasoning
which has been so largely adopted with regard to

Napoleon's actions and intentions at this and other crises of his life. That he was a man of unrivalled energy and resource, that his strategy was incomparably brilliant, that his administrative powers excelled those of other rulers, that he did great things for France, or, according to some, for all Europe; all these may be true of him. But they constitute no valid reason for rejecting the plain method of attaining the historical truth as to his motives and conduct by direct and trustworthy evidence, in order to judge of them by imaginative speculations founded upon his supposed powers and insight.

In this case of Quatre Bras there is not the least occasion to seek other witness than that of Napoleon, for his letters reveal his whole mind. Once lay aside any special prepossessions in favour of the writer, and the state of the case is perfectly manifest. Napoleon had no idea that three-fourths of the Prussians were collected in his front. As he was aware beforehand how their army was cantoned, and judged Blücher still to be near Namur, it follows that he believed himself in contact with their extreme right wing, which unsupported must needs give way, and open his path to Brussels. *Ante, 100; or Orig. in Sib.i.App.; or in Cha. p.115,116. See ante, p. 102.*

As to the English army, the letter already quoted, sent by the officer of lancers, proves that he thought no troops of theirs moving except possibly some of the reserve from Brussels. Slight false alarms previously ordered at points on the western frontier, or false intelligence given Wellington at his instance *See Ibid.*

I

by spies, or Wellington's supposed natural slowness,
may either of them have been his reason for so
judging. We can only know the fact, which was that
he felt sure, when writing to Ney just before leaving
Charleroi, that none of the English corps westward
of Nivelles could yet be moving on Quatre Bras.
Whether to take advantage of the supposed gap, and
push boldly between his enemies to the capital, or to
turn to his right and crush the nearest of the Prussian corps, he did not intend to decide until he had
fairly taken up positions beyond the Fleurus triangle,
and gathered some further information.   In doing
thus much he expected no serious opposition.   Such
are the facts as deduced direct from his own evidence,
which quite sets aside the notion put forward by
Thiers, and originated in one of the St. Helena contradictory versions, that he was intending that afternoon to fight a decisive battle with Blücher before
Wellington arrived, and was purposely allowing the
Prussians to concentrate.

See ante,
p. 102.
See Reply
toRogniat,
Mém. viii.

If there were the least doubt of this it would be
set at rest by the 2 p.m. letter, which proves, beyond
all dispute, to the unprejudiced, that *Napoleon was
even then*, after his own midday reconnaissance of
the Prussians, *unaware of their actual force*.   The
Emperor never wrote on such a point loosely ; and
to suppose that he would describe Blücher's army,
outnumbering his own (without Lobau) by a full
third, as ' un corps de troupes,' and this in writing to
Ney specific instructions as to how to operate, is to

See ante,
p. 104.

claim omniscience for his vision at the expense of gross injustice to his pen. It is only necessary further to say that Thiers wisely gives no evidence in proof Thi. xx.79. of his assertion that the Emperor, on surveying the enemy, 'estimated them at about 90,000 strong.' As his own words to Ney contradict this, it becomes necessary (on the Thiers' assumption that his observation was infallible) to assert first roundly that he guessed the numbers of the Prussians at a number within a small fraction of the truth, and then, since Thi. xx.83. the 2 p.m. letter to Ney cannot quite be passed over, to misquote it thus, ' he had sent Ney a message to announce to him that they were about to attack *the Prussian army established in front of Sombreffe.*' This is the course which the historian has adopted to get over the difficulty. It is hardly necessary to add, that he does not quote the words of the earlier letters at all. In fact, he uses not a line of them which could conflict with his advocacy. But at 3 p.m., when Napoleon had found out the truth, and wrote with corresponding force his pressing note for Ney's aid, it is no longer dangerous to reveal the writer's mind by using his own language, and this one order Ibid. 89. of the five that day given Ney is quoted by the historian at full length !

To touch once more on the question of the alleged clearness and regularity of the staff service of the Grand Army, it is worth noting that in the very detailed letter from Charleroi dictated by the Emperor to supplement Soult's orders, the Marshal is directed

See Orig.
in Cha. p.
115.

particularly how to dispose of his *eight* divisions of infantry, whilst one of the eight (Girard's) was kept away from him (a fact of which his own instructions to Reille and D'Erlon show him uninformed), and employed with Grouchy's wing in front of the Prussians. However this contradiction and careless-ness may be excused, it is not the less strikingly at variance with some popular notions on the subject of Napoleon's infallibility as to details.

This brings us naturally to speak of a curious error in Thiers' history relative to the position of this division on the previous night. It has been mentioned Ante, p. 104. that the name of their quarters is erroneously given in two places by that writer as Wagnelée, instead of Wangenies. Now, the latter place lies a little more than a mile S.W. of Fleurus, and was the natural position of the extreme left of the French advance that night ; but Wagnelée lies three miles more to the north, and therefore almost in rear of the Prussian right during the battle of the next day ; and Girard formed nominally part of the command of Ney, who ought, in the Thiers' view, to have detached troops upon that rear. Hence to those readers who do not detect the error, it seems as though part of Ney's troops were already close to the point required, at nightfall on the 15th. As the fine atlas published for Thiers' history very carefully in two maps distin-guishes between these villages we are led to the in-evitable conclusion, that either the writer has not referred to his own map, or has not done so with the intention of using it for honest illustration of the facts.

We come next to the charge against Ney as to the late hour of the advance on Quatre Bras. This is one of the matters to which Thiers, in common with the whole class he represents, assigns vast importance as regards the result of the day and of the whole campaign. In order here to fix upon Ney a serious responsibility, he has made in his details the following assertions : that it was not until after some considerable delay, and after sending the lancer officer for further instructions, that, ' pressed by reiterated orders, he at last sent Reille and D'Erlon instructions to advance with all speed ; ' that after this he would not begin the action until the time ' when the guns at Ligny thundered heavily, it being now near 3 p.m. ; ' that Bylandt's brigade was not to be (' ne devait pas être ') at Quatre Bras until 2 p.m., or, as he elsewhere puts it, could not be ' entirely ' up till that time ; and that Ney waited, after the fight began, so long for the last division of Reille, as to give time for Picton's succour to appear first and save the Dutch-Belgians. These allegations are preceded by the general and more vague charge, that Ney stood hesitating from morning till near noon before Bernard's 4,000 men.

This last is easily disposed of. It merely means that Ney waited for his orders. There has been shown to be no pretence for believing that he had any instructions to occupy Quatre Bras previous to those sent by Flahault, and that Soult required him to

Thi. xx. 73.
Ibid. 103.

Ibid. 105.
Ibid. 70.
Ibid. 104.

Ibid. 102–3.

Ante, p. 99.
Ante, p. 100, and Orig. Order, Mém. ix. 335.

Ante, p.
112.
report his position previous to these being issued.   In
short, there was no possible reason why Ney should
attack the unknown force in his front more than
Grouchy that on the right.   Had he done so indeed
with the one infantry division in hand, and been un-
successful, the same critics who condemn him for
delay would have blamed him unsparingly for going
before the orders of his master.

As to Ney's alleged delay after the orders arrived,
there is one all-sufficient reply which would settle this
Ante, p.
102.
in his favour, viz., Napoleon's answer to his own single
request for instructions.   Had he adhered literally to
See Orig.
Mém. ix.
337.
this he would not have attacked Quatre Bras at all
until ' he had united the corps of Reille, D'Erlon, and
Kellermann;' in other words, he might have waited for
D'Erlon's arrival, and in that case would not have
been engaged that day.   But, in fact, it is not necessary to plead this.   A consideration of the times and
distances (the latter measured from the very large and
accurate Belgian Government survey) proves abun-
Ante, p.
102.
dantly that the only delay between the passage of
Flahault past Reille's quarters at Gosselies with the
orders, and the advance from Frasnes, was simply the
short loss of time on Reille's part in not starting at
Flahault's instance, but waiting for the direct order
See Orig.
Sib. i. 450.
which was sent promptly back by Ney—as its tenor
proves—as soon as he received the Emperor's instructions.   This would be considerably less than the
time of a horseman between Gosselies and Frasnes
and back, an hour's ride for an aide-de-camp ; for

Reille's report as to the Prussians is not referred to in the narrative of Heymès, nor in the orders sent by Ney, and plainly did not affect the movement, which was simply delayed, as Reille's letter proves, pending the arrival of the latter. 'Instead of commencing any movement,' he wrote, ' after the report of General Girard, I shall hold the troops ready to march, *and await your orders*. As these can get to me very quickly, there will be *only very little time lost*.' Ante, p. 102. See Heymès in Mém. ix. 256. See Orig. Sib. i. 449.

As half an hour would be a very moderate space for getting the two divisions ready, it does not appear that the lost time could have been more than another half; and this not by any choice of Ney, for his lancer messenger had been dispatched (as the time of Napoleon's answer proves) *before* the receipt of the Emperor's letter, and in default of any morning instructions reaching him. So that Thiers' allusion to this message, and his description of Ney's only acting ' under reiterated orders,' prove but parts of a mass of fiction which has been built up to cover the failure of the French strategy for the day. The sole and very brief delay was that shown to be Reille's, which that general foresaw at the moment, and wrote of it, correctly enough, in the terms just quoted. See Orig. Mém. ix. 337.

We need not discuss at any length the time when the action was begun. We have given the plainest evidence from both sides that the hour was not later than 2 p.m. Thiers has tried to show from the journal of General Foy, one of the eye-witnesses, that the cannon of Ligny were heard whilst Ney and Reille Ante, p. 103. Thi. xx. 105

were discussing the advance, and that there was no
real action engaged at Quatre Bras until this quickened
them, but merely some artillery skirmishing. Unfortunately for this proof that Ney was behind Napoleon, which is the only one adduced, its value depends
entirely upon the time that the Ligny firing began.

Thi. xx.
105.

Thiers settles this conclusively to himself by the
simple phrase, ' Now, these guns were only heard at
half-past two at the earliest.'   When we find, however, the distinct statement from the highest Prussian

Pr. Off.
p. 27.

authority that the enemy's light troops were *can-
nonading their own from between eleven and twelve*,
as the latter fell back into the position, we see at
once how the mistake of Foy occurred.   On the

Ante, p.
103.

other hand, the witnesses we have already cited
concur in the distinct assertion, that at Quatre Bras
the French *columns* advanced not later than 2 p.m.
We can afford, therefore, here once more to set
this part of the Thiers' misstatements completely
aside.

For the next we have to consider, the alleged
non-arrival of Bylandt's brigade until far in the day,
there is no excuse.   One battalion, indeed, was left
by orders at Nivelles, but the rest have been shown

Ante, p.
105.

joining the Prince of Orange between 4 and 9 a.m.
The historian who brought Bernard's brigade from

Ante, p.
94.

Nivelles (where they had not been) the day before,
can hardly be expected to take the trouble of inquiring from the Dutch writers how a Dutch brigade
moved on the 16th : but it was scarcely worth while

to use this ignorance of his own against the character of the Marshal.

Lastly, when Ney is accused of not pressing his attack with Foy and Bachelu sufficiently, and of thus giving time for Picton to come in, it is only necessary to point out that the third division of Reille was the Cha.p.156. strongest in the army (numbering, as is admitted, over 7,000 men), that it was following Foy's on to the ground, and that Ney's orders all implied his using it as well as five more which he had not. As in an hour and a half (at the outside limit of the estimated time, from the opening to the arrival of Picton) he had pushed the Prince of Orange back the mile and a half from near Frasnes to Quatre Bras, this would be to any judge of military operations a sufficient answer to the reproach of tactical slackness, even were a less active officer than Ney concerned.

We have taken the pains to examine fully the charges of Thiers, knowing that on close inspection they fall to the ground. At a later moment it can be shown, by high opinion, that the hypothetical oc- Vide p. 129. cupation of Quatre Bras is not so certainly to be assumed the decisive measure which it has been ima- gined ; in short, that there is good reason to assert that it would have little affected the grand result.

It will be observed that Thiers enables Napoleon to discover the exact number of the Prussians at Ante, p. 115. Ligny, and that, be it remembered, by a reconnais- sance made after the skirmishing had begun. That Thiers is here again romancing has been shown from

Napoleon's own orders ; but it is as well to remark, that the impossibility of such an estimate is well shown by what went on on the other side, where Wellington, Blücher, and their staffs assembled at Bry. All took the wing of Napoleon's army before them for the whole, and looked on any troops on the Quatre Bras side as a mere detachment. In accordance with this view we find Blücher (as honest-minded a writer in such matters as any in modern history) reporting the army that attacked him as consisting of 130,000 men, that being in fact the estimate of the Grand Army previously gained through spies, and supposed by him to be more accurate than any guess made by a distant and partly smoke-obscured view.

Ante, p. 106.

Doc. 89.

Ante, p. 40.

Much comment is not necessary on the failure of Wellington in his promised co-operation, more especially as we have the distinct assurance of Müffling that this promise was conditional. The failure was evidently a necessary consequence of the deliberate or over-cautious strategy which marked all the Duke's arrangements during the opening hours of the campaign. To criticise the tactics employed at Ligny hardly comes within the scope of this work ; and it is sufficient to say that it was lost by Blücher against inferior numbers, and that Prussian critics condemn his extended front and his little use of Thielemann. But neither Wellington nor Blücher could possibly tell that Napoleon would abstain from bringing up 10,000 of his army (Lobau) from some doubt on his own mind as to the actual force of the Prussians, and lose 20,000

Ante, p. 106.

Müff. Hist. 70, 71.
Claus. p. 89, &c.

more (D'Erlon) by want of concert with his lieutenants.   Had it not been for these mistakes of his,
the blow to the Prussian army might obviously have
been far more serious than it was, and the absence of
their Allies more dangerously felt.

It was quite in accordance with the extreme caution with which Wellington acted the day before, that
Picton's, the leading division of the reserve, should
have been halted some hours at Waterloo, where the
Nivelles and Quatre Bras roads from Brussels divide.
This halt has provoked much comment ; as that of Claus. p.
Clausewitz, who believes that Wellington purposely $^{101.}$
left Picton there until after his meeting with Blücher
at Bry—a supposition obviously inconsistent with the
known time of Picton's appearance.   This attack has
produced, on the Duke's side, a not less inaccurate Reply to
contradiction of the fact of the halt, and an assertion Supp.
that his reserve came up ' about mid-day ; ' statements x. 525.
which cause regret that he only gave heed to criticism
when so old and so far removed from the events as
to have lost the memory of their details.   Siborne gives Sib. i. 102.
very completely the circumstances and reason of the
halt, and these agree so exactly with the distances
from Brussels to Waterloo and Waterloo to Quatre
Bras, and the times of the beginning and end of the
march, as to   leave no doubt that he is correct.
Numerous letters from persons in the division, written Doc. 72,
just after the events, put the movement from Brussels &c.
at from 1 to 2 a.m. and the arrival at Quatre Bras at
3 p.m.   It is obvious that a division of good troops

under an officer of Picton's character, with fine weather
and a first-class chaussée to move on, could not have
spent thirteen hours in passing over twenty-one miles
without some special cause of delay : and the halt at
Waterloo has been the only cause ever assigned for
the late arrival on the field where their support was
so urgently needed.

Thi. xx.63.
Cha.p.118.
Thiers and Charras agree that it was by the Emperor's choice that Lobau was left for many hours close
to Charleroi, in uncertainty as to whether he was
ultimately to follow Ney's wing (which he had power
to do if he judged it best), or to support Napoleon.
In accordance with the custom of the latter historian,
he takes care to prove this by the original testimony of
Thi. xx.63.
Cha. p.
118, n.
Colonel Janin. The uncertainty arose very probably
from the mistake, so often before mentioned, which
the Emperor lay under with regard to the Prussians ;
or possibly this hesitating strategy may have been but
part of the fruit of the doubt and uneasiness which
he himself confesses in a noteworthy passage of the
Quin. p.
119.
' Mémorial ' (of Las Cases) which Quinet has brought
into special prominence. If this be trustworthy evidence, and Napoleon really said to his St. Helena
confidant, ' What is certain is, that I had no longer
within myself the feeling of decided success,' much
comment on his indecision would be superfluous.
Viewed in any light, the Napoleon who left Lobau to
choose which wing of the army he would join, was not
the Napoleon of Rivoli, of Wagram, or even of Lutzen.

Though his powers were possibly not lessened, his faith On this see note at end of Lect. II.
in his own star must have grown weaker.

The wandering of D'Erlon's corps has naturally
attracted as much critical remark as any other single
point in the campaign. The facts already given are
undisputed. It remains therefore to ascertain by
whose orders the corps was withdrawn from Ney's
rear, and by whose sanction sent back from the Ligny
side, and again restored to the Marshal too late to be
of service.

Ney, it is admitted, had nothing to do with the
first cross-movement. It must have been consequent
on (1) an order of Napoleon's, or (2) a suggestion of
D'Erlon's own, or (3) the error of some inferior officer.
The first of these is the view of M. Thiers, who has
taken vast pains to make the world believe that
D'Erlon's march was the result of deep forethought
on the part of the Emperor, and was commanded by a
special missive, shown afterwards to Ney, and borne by
Labedoyère. From this he goes on to use such ex-
pressions as, 'les ordres réitérés de Napoléon,' and, Thi. xx. 97, 100.
'D'Erlon tant appelé, tant attendu.' The astonished
reader has a natural difficulty in seeing any reason
why Napoleon, after all this trouble taken, should have
let D'Erlon slip away ; but the graceful style of the
historian, and the pretty details which he throws in of
the soldiers 'who clapped their hands on perceiving
themselves* on the Prussian rear,' and 'were thrown Ibid. 123.

---

* Thiers, as well as other writers, speaks of D'Erlon as moving
by the 'Old Roman Road' (or Brunhild Way, as it is locally

into despair by finding themselves turned off from the road which offered such splendid results,' may well blind the unwary to the fact, that the whole of this is no more nor less than a fiction, *directly contradicted by the evidence of Napoleon himself*, on this head an irrefragable witness.

Cha. p.171, et seq.

Charras has examined the D'Erlon question fully, in the light of the ' *Documents inédits*,' published by Ney's son, and has established on their evidence the fact, that the corps was turned off by an excess of

Ante, p. 107.

zeal on the part of an aide-de-camp, carrying the original or duplicate of one of the extant orders of

See his statement, Cha. p.175.

Napoleon, that of a quarter-past 3, already cited.   No fresh order ever reached Ney for such an oblique movement as that made ; and it is no wonder that D'Erlon doubted whether he ought to have obeyed Labedoyère's direction, nor that the Marshal indig-

See Napoleon's words on next page. Claus. p. 98.

nantly recalled the troops which his written instructions clearly prove *he was first to use to carry Quatre Bras before making any detachment to his right*.   Clausewitz, on less perfect evidence, but with his usual insight, had already arrived unhesitatingly at the same

Thi. xx. 135.

conclusion.   Thiers, writing after Charras, has taken

See Map.

named), which leads across the Fleurus triangle from the Quatre Bras Road towards the Prussian rear, *as if this were the only available path for such a flank march.* The simple fact is, that the fields

See p. 125.

in the triangle are intersected by numerous cart-roads quite available for troops in such fine weather as D'Erlon had. The particular one used would, from Napoleon's description of the appearance of the corps, be that leading from the village of Mellet towards Fleurus, and so on the French rear, not the Prussian. But this ' Roman Road' notion is but one touch of many to aid in the deception of the D'Erlon myth.

much pains to combat this view ; but his witnesses, D'Erlon and one of the generals under him, only prove that *they supposed* the aide-de-camp to be acting by Napoleon's authority. Now, what has Napoleon said of this himself (whom Thiers has told us to be the most veracious of contemporary writers) in the early narrative, admitted to be the most faithful of those he put forth at St. Helena ? We will quote his own words, merely calling attention to the fact that, had he really sent the order for the movement which Ney thus set aside, no possible reason could exist why it should be concealed to the damage of the writer's own fame. 'Vandamme sent to report that an enemy's column, 20,000 strong, was debouching from the woods and thus *turning us,* heading apparently for Fleurus. [It is at this point in the Thiers story that the soldiers *have gained the Prussian rear,* and are applauding the Emperor's foresight.] At half-past six, Dejean came and announced that this was the 1st Corps commanded by D'Erlon. *Napoleon could assign no reason for such a movement.'* Not a word is added of any order sent thereupon to D'Erlon by the Emperor, and his name is no further mentioned in the narrative of the battle of Ligny. Gourg. p. 50.

In some remarks further on, Napoleon adds, ' The movements of the 1st Corps are difficult to explain. Did Ney misunderstand the order to make, WHEN MASTER OF QUATRE BRAS, a diversion on the rear of the Prussians ? Or did D'Erlon, between Gosselies and Frasnes, hearing a hot cannonade to his right, and Ibid. p. 56.

none from Quatre Bras, conceive that he ought to move upon the cannonade which he would have left behind him, if he followed the main road onward ? With this clear and distinct statement we may forbear to follow the details of a controversy, where controversy is out of place. Thiers makes Napoleon our best evidence, and on this point there is good reason to believe he is so. Let us be content to acquit him of what he evidently in 1816 believed the mistake of some subordinate, and not imagine for him a strategical stroke of which he knew nothing.

Gourg. p. 57.

His testimony is no less satisfactory as to the return of D'Erlon towards Ney, of which he simply says, ' it was another false movement of this corps to do this, when informed of St. Armand being carried.' Not the least allusion is made to *any order of his own to stay*, though had such been given and disobeyed, the incompleteness of his own victory would have had excellent excuse. In plain fact, it is apparent he had not called D'Erlon's corps up, and did not forbid its return to the point on which he had originally ordered it. Thiers, on the testimony of one of the division generals of the corps, that D'Erlon went off in spite of

Thi. xx. 138, *n*.

' *nouvelles instances de la droite*,' would have it that, in so acting on Ney's pressure, he disregarded Napoleon's wish. Napoleon's own criticisms, we may be sure, would have told us had this been so. The ' fresh instances ' were not his, it appears from his own narrative ; and had he really ordered, we may be quite sure D'Erlon knew his first duty, and would have

promptly obeyed.　As Charras has well remarked, the Cha.p.174.
mistake of the aide-de-camp alone reconciles the testimony as to the first movement, the consent of Napoleon that as to the second one, which together neutra-
lised the corps for the day.

Of the tactical faults of Blücher it is not necessary Ante, p. 122.
to speak further ; and his strategical mistake at the
outset, the loss of Bülow by imperfect orders, has Ante, p. 95.
been fully noticed before.　Of Wellington, viewed individually, it is sufficient to say that his enemy, had
matters been properly managed, should have attacked
him with 20,000 men more, early in the afternoon ; and
that he at dark, thirty hours after his first warning, had
only present at Quatre Bras *three-eighths* of his infantry, *one-third* of his guns, and *one-seventh* of his
cavalry.　Truly, in holding his own, the great English- See Table, Sib. i. 153.
man owed something that day to Fortune.

Here, however, arises a larger question ; for much
of the pile of literature on this day's affairs owes its
origin to the supposed importance of the position of
Quatre Bras.　Now, this importance, in the sense
usually meant, is by no means uncontested.　In saying
this, we offer no opinion of our own, but point to that
of Clausewitz, a critic by no means too favourable, it is
believed, to the side of Wellington.　The sum of the
observations, in which he has exhaustively treated the Claus. p. 103–107.
question, is that Ney could not have pushed on alone
between the Allies without an unreasonable risk ; that
his advancing could not have prevented Wellington
from uniting his army at some point beyond ; that in

K

occupying the English general fully he fulfilled his proper task for the day ; and that his 'wheeling against the Prussians' was a mere second-thought of Napoleon's, which assumed mistakenly that he would have no serious opposition at Quatre Bras, and was ordered too late for any possible accomplishment.

In this question of time the view of the great German critic approaches that of Charras, who has shown
Cha.p.114. that the delay of Napoleon in the morning was the original cause of the incompleteness of his operations for the day.　According to Clausewitz's summing up,
Claus. p. 107. 'This whole outcry against Ney, on the side of Bonaparte, is but the wish to represent his own plan as more brilliant and grand than it actually was at the time of the transaction.　What Ney might have done we all see *now*, when all the accidents are known which could not have been reckoned on then.　The same critic, however, rating the French army lower than does their countryman, has declared that their position on the night before showed of itself that they could not be brought up and engaged at Sombreffe before the
Ibid. p. 58. afternoon of the 16th.

Summary.

Leaving the mazes of controversy once more to note the proven facts of the day, it appears that Napoleon's troops had no orders, beyond the completion of the movement across the river, until seven or eight hours of daylight had passed away, and the Prussians had collected three-fourths of their army to do him battle.

Also that his morning orders clearly prove that he expected no serious opposition from them or the English at present, and was divided only in his mind between the thought of pressing on direct to Brussels between the two Allied armies, or striking at the supposed Prussian right, driven back on Fleurus the day before. That, his orders once issued, there was no delay on Ney's part, though the appearance of the Prussians did detain Reille's two rear divisions about half an hour on their move from Gosselies. That Ney exceeded his orders in committing himself to a decisive action with these and Bachelu's divisions only present of eight which he had been told to unite for the purpose. That D'Erlon, having been left until 11 a.m. in rear of Gosselies, was late in coming up, and was turned off towards Napoleon's flank by the mistake of an aide-de-camp, when he should have gone on first to Quatre Bras, whither he afterwards arrived by a second cross-march by Ney's order, and the tacit consent of the Emperor, yet too late to be of service. That, in consequence of his absence, Ney was finally outnumbered at Quatre Bras, and driven back on Frasnes. That the Allies this day, owing to the Bülow mistake and Wellington's deliberation, only brought into action *forces actually less than Napoleon's army*, but that Napoleon's reserving Lobau, and missing D'Erlon, caused him to fight at both points of contact with inferior numbers. That Ney's action was so far important that Wellington found it entirely impossible to support Blücher as he had at noon intended. That Wellington nearly lost

See further, Ney's letter, Doc. 150.

K 2

the cross-roads at first, because his continued anxiety in the morning as to his right caused him to delay bringing up the Reserve, which might have reached Quatre Bras easily before Ney attacked. That Blücher was defeated owing to Bülow's absence and the superior tactics of Napoleon. Lastly, that the Allied mistakes were at once redeemed by the bold order which Gneisenau gave for a retreat on Wavre ; for, in thus giving up the proper line of communication of the Prussians through Namur and Liège, he, at the risk of present inconvenience, kept moving parallel to the road by which Wellington must retire, and so gave the armies that precious opportunity of aiding each other in battle, which they had missed on the plain of Fleurus. This noble daring at once snatched from Napoleon the hoped-for fruits of his victory, and the danger Ligny had for a few hours averted was left impending over him. The sequel will show how completely the strategy which followed exceeded Napoleon's conception of the vigour of his enemies, so that his own want of insight into their new combination made complete the triumph they prepared.

LECTURE V.

EVENTS OF THE 17TH.—COMMENTS.—SUMMARY.

NAPOLEON has told us with elaborate pains, in more than one narrative, that his knowledge of the characters of the Allied generals made him both desirous to deal with Blücher first, and confident that that commander would give him the earliest opportunity of battle.   If this were his actual calculation at the time, it was remarkably justified by the event; for we have seen that the attack on 85,000 Prussians at Ligny was begun when but two divisions of Wellington's army were assembled at Quatre Bras ; and that a victory was actually won over the former, whilst their allies, though not worsted, were at any rate so occupied by Ney, and so slow in gathering, as to be unable to afford Blücher the least assistance.   The first part of the French programme, as afterwards published from St. Helena, had therefore not failed.   What, it remains to be asked, was the further advantage which the Emperor had hoped to gain by this partial success at the outset ?

To understand his anticipations it is only necessary to remember that, the natural base of supply for the

Gourg. p. 63. Mém. ix. 69.

Prussian army being the Lower Rhine, their commu-
See Map. nication to it from the Fleurus country would turn due
eastward through Namur and Liège ; while that of
Wellington's army, if collected in the same district,
would pass northward by or near Brussels to the
seaports of Antwerp and Ostend, which connected it
with England.　These lines would meet in fact at a
right angle, the apex of which was the cross-roads of
Quatre Bras.　If either of the two armies should begin
to retire along the line which led to its respective base,
it would at once be separating from the other ; and
every mile of direct retreat would give so much the
larger opening between their flanks, and thus increase
the chances of a French army desiring to deal singly
with them.　This was no supposititious case.　In 1794
the Austrians, acting on the same line as Blücher now,
and defeated on nearly the same ground in the battle
of Fleurus, commenced a retreat towards the Rhine,
which soon carried them away from their English and
Dutch allies under the Duke of York; and their so
doing gave a decided advantage to the French invaders
of Belgium, which from that hour was never lost.
Napoleon was too close a student of the revolutionary
See his
letter to
Ney to be
quoted
presently. wars not to be fully aware of these facts.　It seemed
to him, as the sequel shows, more than probable that
whichever of the Allies was defeated would be naturally tempted to imitate the Austrian general of twenty
years before, and secure his own direct retreat.　He
knew Blücher was too practical a soldier not to re-
cognise the immense inconvenience which it would be,

in case of prolonged hostilities, to abandon the Namur-
Liège line, and open a new one from Prussia to supply
his army by. This knowledge, added to his naturally
sanguine temperament, made him calculate at once,
after Ligny was won, that the natural result would be
that separation of his enemies which he desired, by the
retirement eastward of the defeated army. Hope and
imagination went hand-in-hand with Napoleon, and it
is not surprising, therefore, that we find him writing
his first letter to Ney on the morning of the 17th in the See Orig.
Sib. i. 457.
following positive terms : ' The Prussian army has been
put to the rout ; General Pajol is pursuing it on the
roads to Namur and Liège.'

The real movements of the Prussians were very
different. As has been before mentioned, Gneisenau,
coming into temporary command after the fall of
Blücher at the end of the battle, and finding the
struggle for the present hopelessly decided, chose at
all risk of inconvenience to abstain from the notion
of a retreat to the east, and to keep as near as might
be to the English army. Without any further communication with Wellington (for the failure of Major See p. 109.
Winterfeldt's mission to that general was not guessed
at), he put his army in motion northward for Wavre
at the earliest daybreak. Bülow, who had only heard
of his own mistake in delaying his march, at Hannut,
at 10 a.m. on the morning of the battle, had in Pr. Off.
p. 18.
vain hurried his men along the old Roman road
(that mentioned before as the Brunhild Way), which
leads direct from that place, by the field of Ramillies,

to Marbais near Ligny. At nightfall his leading
Pr. Off.
p. 20.
See Map.
division had not attained Gembloux by three miles,
when it halted near Sauvenière after an exhausting
march.

The order of the Prussian retreat was simple
enough, and was neither molested nor even noticed
See p. 135.
by the French, as Napoleon's own words show.
Pr. Off.
p. 54.
Zieten left the vicinity of the Ligny plateau at daybreak, and by field tracks made his way due northward through the villages of Tilly, Gentinnes, and
Mont St. Guibert to Wavre, where he crossed the Dyle
to the further side of the town. A little later Pirch
followed him, halting, however, on the south side of
Wavre, and leaving detachments to cover their rear.
Thielemann, who had the reserve parks of the army
in charge, moved separately and more slowly, going
Ibid. p. 55.
through Gembloux (which he only quitted at 2 p.m.),
and reaching Wavre so late that he could not carry
his whole corps through the town that night to
the north bank of the Dyle, as had been intended.
Bülow made a march (in accordance with distinct
instructions received that morning) by the villages of
Walhain and Corbaix to that of Dion-le-Mont, three
miles S.E. of Wavre, where he took up a position,
with strong rearguards thrown out to relieve those of
Pirch, and cover from any pursuit of the French the
army thus happily concentrated.

Between the road from Gembloux to Wavre, and
that from Quatre Bras to Waterloo, the country is
cut up by the various heads of the river Dyle, each

making a deep valley with marshy meadows on the
streams, and rendering military movements across the
district difficult. Hence a more direct attempt to get
near to Wellington would have been inappropriate to
Gneisenau's purpose, as it would have also had the
obvious objection of carrying the beaten corps away
from an immediate junction with the important rein- Müff. Hist.
p. 10.
forcement of Bülow. To march on Wavre combined
the present object of uniting this to the rest of the
army, with the coming one of being within supporting
distance of Wellington. The day's movements proved
the soundness of the first calculation, as those of the
18th were to crown the second.

We have left Wellington the winner of the action
at Quatre Bras, but with only 30,000 of his army
(partly of the Prince of Orange's corps, partly of
the Reserve) on the ground, and these largely reduced
by their hot day's work. They were raised to about
45,000 strong by the arrival of the cavalry and of
the rest of the Reserve during the night, or very
early in the morning; but Chassé's division of the Loben S.
p. 234.
Prince of Orange's corps was left at Nivelles for
lack of orders, and none of Lord Hill's corps were See Map.
nearer than that place, part of one of his two English
divisions, Colville's, being on their way to it by
Braine-le-Comte, and the Dutch-Belgians of the Corps
under Prince Frederick being still further off at
Enghien. Wellington's orders written at Genappe, Gur. xii.
475.
where he slept, sufficiently show him quite unconscious of the Prussian intentions, and anxious to

complete the concentration at Quatre Bras ; but he rode early back to the scene of the action of the 16th, and soon learnt the truth. An aide-de-camp with an escort communicated early with General Zieten, and heard what Gneisenau had ordered ; and before the English troops had cooked their breakfast an officer from Blücher's own headquarters, already moved to Wavre, brought messages from the Marshal. A retreat was of course essential in Wellington's exposed position ; but the line taken by the Prussians, and the failure (which Wellington observed) of the French to pursue, spoke so plainly of a prospect of cordial co-operation leading to victory, that the Duke at once announced his intention of pausing in his movement on Brussels, to accept battle in the position of Waterloo (reconnoitred and reported on for him the year before), provided Blücher would help him with part of his army. Covered by Alten's division (of the Prince of Orange's Corps), and the cavalry, the retreat of the English main body was begun in excellent order, and continued throughout the day until completed. Lord Hill led direct to Waterloo the troops from Nivelles, Chassé's and Clinton's divisions and part of Colville's. The rest of Colville's and Frederick's Dutch-Belgians moved by a third road from Enghien on Hal, a town ten miles westward of Waterloo, where they were ordered to halt, to cover Brussels on that side. With the exception of this detachment and a single brigade marching up from Ghent to arrive at daylight, the

Marginal notes:

Supp. Disp. x. 527. Mu. Mem. p. 240.

Ibid. p. 241.

Supp. Disp. x. 527.

Mü. Mem. p. 241.

Müff. Hist. p. 16. See Mem. on defence of Netherlands, dated 22nd Sept. 1814. Gur. xii. 129.

Loben S. p. 233. Gur. xii. p. 475.

Müff. Hist. p. 14. Sib. i. 279.

whole fighting army of Wellington lay that night
upon the ground which the next day was to make
the most famous battlefield in the world.   Their
left was but seven miles distant, in a straight line,
from the right of their allies at Bierge, near Wavre ;
and their chief, in reply to his demand for aid, had
received from Blücher, now fully recovered, the
characteristic reply, ' he would march with his whole   Muff. Hist.
army to join him, and if the French delayed to   p. 16.
attack, the Allies would give them battle on the   Pr. Off.
                                                    p. 53.
19th.'   The Prussians, thrown off their line of
supply, and having brought but slender rations with
them, were short of food already ; but the ' zeal of the
troops,' says the official writer, ' was not slackened,'   Ibid. p. 55.
and their conduct next day fully justifies this boast.
As it was necessary to take immediate steps to re-   Müff. Hist.
place the abandoned line of supply, all heavy baggage   p. 71.
was directed next morning on Louvain, through   Pr. Off.
which city the new line was already ordered to be   p. 58.
                                                    Claus. p.
opened.   112.

The chief interest of this day's proceedings again
reverts to Napoleon, the central figure of the drama.
As we now know fully what the Prussians were doing
in the early morning, we may better judge how entirely
he deceived himself as to the extent of his victory and
its consequences.   It was not before 7, and by most   Thi. xx.
reports past 8 a.m. on the 17th, that he first left his   146.
                                                         Cha. p.188.
quarters at Fleurus to visit the battlefield and review
his victorious troops.   His whole mind at that hour is
revealed by the letter to Ney, which he dictated before

starting for Bry, and which replied in detail to the
message sent by that Marshal for instructions through
General Flahault, the bearer of the morning orders of
the day before. Flahault reported Ney yet uncertain
of the results of the battle of Ligny. Soult, writing
for the Emperor, said, ' I thought I had already acquainted you with the victory gained. The Prussian
army has been put to the rout; General Pajol [who
took with him half of one of the four cavalry corps]
is pursuing them on the roads to Namur and Liège.
Some thousands of prisoners have been taken, and
thirty pieces of cannon. . . . The Emperor is going to
Bry, and, as it is possible the English army may act
in your front, he would in that case march directly
against it by the Quatre Bras road, whilst you attack
it in front with your division, which at present ought
to be united. You must report your exact position,
and what goes on in your front. Yesterday the
Emperor remarked with regret that your divisions
acted separately. If the corps of D'Erlon and Reille
had been kept together, not an Englishman would have
escaped. If Count D'Erlon had executed the movement on St. Amand that the Emperor had ordered,
the Prussian army would have been totally destroyed.
Keep your troops together on a league of ground,
well in hand.

' His Majesty's intention is that you take up a position at Quatre Bras as you were ordered ; but if it is
impossible to do that, send a detailed report immediately, and the Emperor will move thither. *If, on the*

See Orig.
in Mém. ix.
340, or in
Sib. i. App.

contrary, there is only a rearguard, drive it off and occupy the position.

'To-day is required for completing this operation' (whether Napoleon's or Ney's is not clear, even to the French editor of the 'Mémoires'), 'filling up ammunition, and gathering stragglers and detachments. Give the necessary orders, and see that all the wounded are sent to the rear.' The letter closes with a report from a Prussian prisoner that their army was lost.

See Note, Mém. ix. 341.

We have followed the text of this famous dispatch nearly entire, for the purpose of comparing it by-and-by with the version Thiers gives of it, and with the references to the subject in Napoleon's own narrative.

The orders to Ney dispatched, the Emperor betook himself by carriage to Ligny, and there, mounting his horse, reviewed and addressed his troops by turns. Lobau's corps (reduced by a division, Teste's, detached to support General Pajol), not having been engaged on the 16th, was pushed on at 10 a.m.* from the plateau of Bry towards Quatre Bras, followed by the Guard an hour later. Meanwhile, Napoleon, either waiting for their movement to go forward, or not recognising the importance of the hours, not only addressed the Prussian prisoners at some length, but 'conversed with his generals on the most various subjects—war, policy, the parties that divided France, the Royalists and Jacobins—appearing very satisfied with the work of the last two days, and hoping yet more from those

Thi. xx. 146. Cha.p.188.

Ibid. and Thi. xx. 102.

Cha.p.188. Thi. xx. 149 (from which last this extract)

---

* So Charras; and Thiers (pp. 153, 154) says of Napoleon, 'Vers onze heures il quitta Bry. Il trouva Lobau en pleine marche,' &c.

which were to follow.'   Hearing from his reconnoitring
Cha.p.189.
Thi. xx.
150. parties that the English were yet at Quatre Bras, he
wrote further brief instructions to Ney, dated ' Before
Ligny, noon, the 17th,' and running thus :

See Orig.
Cha.p.189,
or Sib. i.
459.   ' The Emperor has just placed in position before
Marbais a corps of infantry and the Imperial Guard.
His Majesty desires me to tell you, that his intention is
that you should attack the enemy at Quatre Bras, and
drive them from their position, and that the corps at
Marbais should second your operations.   His Majesty
is going to Marbais, and waits impatiently for your
report.'   It was after writing this letter, as the authors
on each side agree, that he called Grouchy to his side,
and confided to his charge a large detachment,* comprising 33,000 men of all arms, with certain verbal
instructions, on the precise tenor of which the evidence
is not wholly reconcilable, but which certainly implied
Thi. xx.
152.
Cha.p.191. that he was to pursue the Prussians, complete their
defeat, and communicate constantly with Napoleon by
the Namur road.

Grouchy little liked so vague a charge with such
critical responsibility, and expressed his mind freely as
Ib. & ib. to the difficulty of discovering the Prussians with their
long start in advance; but, after some remonstrance,

---

* Grouchy's actual command (Cha. p. 190, or Thi. xx. 152) :

Vandamme	13,400
Gérard	12,200
Cavalry of Pajol (half corps) .	1,300
Do. of Exelmans . . .	3,100
Teste's division of (Lobau) .	3,000

33,000 with 96 guns.

the Emperor left him to his duty and started for
Marbais and Quatre Bras. From near the former
place (according to Thiers), or from Ligny, General
Bertrand, in Soult's absence, wrote positive instructions for Grouchy's guidance. That Marshal was now
directed to march on Gembloux, for Napoleon had just
received cavalry reports sufficient to alter his belief
that the Prussians were flying to Namur. He was,
however, to reconnoitre the Namur road, to pursue
the enemy, and find out and report what he was doing,
especially with a view to ascertain whether ' he was
separating from the English, or bent on uniting with
them to save Brussels, and try the fate of another
battle.' Such was the whole tenor of this important
letter, which serves to show two things only : that
Napoleon was now uncertain of the line of Blücher's
retreat, and that he judged Gembloux a good point to
move Grouchy on in any case. The cavalry of Exelmans were accordingly soon marched to Gembloux ;
but the infantry of Vandamme and Gérard, which had
been allowed to disperse in order to cook and clean
their arms, were long in moving off. The rain came
down in torrents from 2 p.m. for the remainder of the
day. The road from Sombreffe to Gembloux was, at
that time, but a narrow lane, soon rendered almost impassable for guns, and, as we learn from the testimony
of Gérard, it was 10 p.m. before the tail of the column,
which he brought up, arrived at its bivouac near the
latter place. Here Grouchy had been, for some hours,
searching for intelligence, but could apparently obtain

Thi. xx.
156.
Cha.p.192.

Ibid.
Also
Loben S.
p. 228(who
refers to
the report
of Berton
the Cav.
General).

Thi. xx.
173.
Cha.p.193.
(where
Gérard's
report is
quoted).
Persl.
Obsn.

none certain either from Exelmans, whose cavalry had
Ante,
p. 136,
and Map. reconnoitred as far as Sauvenière (Bülow's halting-
place of the night before), or from Pajol, who spent the
afternoon in the vicinity of the Namur road, where he
had captured some guns and a number of stragglers.
At 10 p.m., the Marshal reported his proceedings to
the Emperor in a letter which displays fully his uncertainty as to the actual doings of the Prussians. ' I
have occupied Gembloux, with my cavalry at Sauvenière. The enemy, to the number of 30,000 men [the
corps of Thielemann, in fact] continue their retreat.
They appear to have divided at Sauvenière into three
See Orig.
Sib. i. 297
Cha.p.194. columns, one going to Wavre by Sart-les-Walhain (a
village northward from Gembloux), one to Perwez
(a village to the north-east). One may perhaps infer,
that a part is going to join Wellington, the centre
under Blücher to retire on Liège, another column with
guns having retreated on Namur. Detachments of
cavalry are being pushed by General Exelmans on
Perwez and Sart-les-Walhain. Acting on their report,
if the mass of the Prussians is retiring on Wavre, I shall
follow them to prevent them from gaining Brussels,
and separate them from Wellington. If my information proves that their principal force has marched to
Perwez, I shall pursue them by that place.' At 2 a.m.
that night Grouchy had made up his mind that Wavre,
and not Perwez, was the line to take. He addressed a
letter to Napoleon, which is not extant, but the chief
contents of which are made clearly known from the
answer of Napoleon, who begins one next day in

reply : ' You have written this morning at 2, that you See Orig.
would march on Sart-les-Walhain ; ' as well as from Claus.
p. 148, or
Grouchy's orders to Vandamme, which the industry of Cha.p.228.
Charras disinterred from the French archives, and
which direct the latter general to move at 6 a.m. on
the above-named place, Gérard being commanded to
follow him. ' I think we shall go further than this
village,' are part of the words ; and it is added that
Pajol was to follow the movement, by marching from
Mazy (on the Namur road) to Grand Leez, a hamlet
nearly due east of Sauvenière, and but two miles
from it.

Quitting Grouchy at this point, preparing for his
next day's work, it remains now only to follow the
Emperor himself through the 17th. We left him
issuing orders near Marbais, with Lobau and the
Guard advancing to Quatre Bras, to take the English
army in flank. But it was now already past noon,
and Wellington well advanced in his retreat on
Waterloo. Napoleon's reinforcements, including a
large body of cavalry, raised the left wing of the
French, deducting losses and Girard's division left at
Ligny, to near 72,000 men with 240 guns.* There Thi. xx.
155.
Cha.p.190.
Note.

* Viz. D'Erlon	20,000
Reille	16,000
Lobau (deducting Teste) . .	7,000
Guard	19,000
Domon (Cavalry of Vandamme)	1,000
Subervie (half Pajol's corps) .	1,500
Milhaud's cavalry corps . .	3,500
Kellermann's cavalry corps .	3,500
	———
	71,500

was no incident of importance in the advance in pursuit of the English, save one sharp skirmish at Genappe, where Lord Uxbridge had to turn and drive back with his household brigade of heavy cavalry Sib. i. 272. some lancers who pressed the 7th Hussars, Wellington's extreme rear, with some vivacity. This repulse, or (according to some accounts) the rain Thi. xx. which fell in torrents all the evening, saved the Eng-160. lish army further interruption until the French reached at dusk the heights of Belle Alliance, opposite Wel-Ibid. 161. lington's chosen position. A deployment of Milhaud's Cha. p. 200. cavalry, which Napoleon here ordered, soon produced such a fire of artillery as convinced him that his enemy was not retiring, as he had feared, through the forest of Soignies under cover of the coming night. The French were halted, therefore, as they came up, and placed in bivouac to await the events of that morrow from which their chief hoped so much, but which was in truth to leave the Emperor and Grand Army nothing but the fame of the past glories they had shared.

Comments.

Those who prefer to judge of Napoleon's proceedings by rules not made for other mortals may take for serious truth certain assertions of the ' Mémoires,' Mém. ix. that Ney was ordered on Quatre Bras ' at break of 94. day,' and Grouchy started on his mission so early that Ibid. 99, 100. he was at Gembloux at 4 p.m., and could have pursued the Prussians flying beyond it at his pleasure that evening. Thiers, who has not accepted the former of these fictions literally, and, as we shall see presently, rejects the latter from his narrative, yet asserts of the Emperor (what is quite as unreal and as inconsistent with his own orders), that, although receiving from Pajol reports of fugitives and guns on the Namur road, he ' did not at all believe in any such resolutions on the part of the Prussians as their seeking to regain the Rhine, leaving the English to rest upon the sea.' To confute such notions of Napoleon's superhuman instinct, we have but to point to his own positive words in the morning letter to Ney, which are as frank on the subject as anything ever written. Up to the time of the order written about noon to Grouchy, there is not a tittle of evidence to show that he changed the view then adopted, which was simply that of an over-sanguine man, who both counted the victory of the 16th more decided than it had been, and reckoned on its being at once followed by strategical results in accordance with his own brightest hope, the separation of the Allies.

The same letter at once in a line absolves Ney from all the charges of hesitation, delay, and disobeying reiterated orders, which Thiers (here following the view of the ' Mémoires ') would heap upon him for not attacking Quatre Bras early in the morning. That Wellington did not begin to move his troops off until about 10 a.m. is a point proved by the united testimony of independent witnesses. Until that hour, therefore, he stood facing Ney with the force

Thi. xx. 155, 156.

See ante, pp. 139, 140.

Thi. xx. 156, 157.

Mém. ix. 96.

Mü. Mem. p. 251. Austrian Report on Campaign. Doc. 101.

victorious the night before, and now reinforced largely.

See trans. of letter, ante, pp. 140, 141.

The words of the morning letter to Ney, ' Si, au contraire, il n'y a qu'une arrière-garde, attaquez-la et prenez position,' are incontrovertible evidence—if there be any meaning at all in them—that *if there were more than a rearguard* before the Marshal, *he was not to attack* and take position, but wait for the promised co-operation from Ligny. The very next sentence to that we have quoted says distinctly that the day was necessary ' to complete this operation,

Ibid.

fill up ammunition, and gather stragglers and detach-ments.' Whoever reads these words with unbiassed view, sees at once that the man who wrote them at 7 or 8 a.m. had no notion of any prolonged pursuit that day. No lengthy argument could so effectually, as these simple sentences, shatter the theory which Thiers has boldly built up at this point. According

Thi. xx. 144.

to this, Napoleon, early in the morning, laid out his plans to press the English to battle that day on the Waterloo ground, should they stand and accept it, instead of retreating through the forest of Soignies ; and he only delayed moving up from Ligny the troops he was to take with him, because willing to give time for Ney's command to march through Quatre Bras first, and for the Guard (who had been engaged late the night before) to finish their rest and meal. In order to support this invention, it was necessary for the historian, writing with the letter to Ney before

Ibid.

him, to say of its purport, ' he enjoined him to march boldly and without loss of time to Quatre Bras,' words

which the original at a glance is seen to refute, with Ante, p. 140.
the rest of the story ; inasmuch as, in the special case
which happened—the non-retreat of the English army
before the instructions reached Ney—' The Emperor,'
it is said, ' would march directly against it by the
Quatre Bras road,' a movement of co-operation for
which Ney was to wait, as he was to attack if the
enemy showed nothing but a rearguard. Heymès, Mém. ix. 261.
who was with Ney all this day, has contradicted in the
flattest manner the notion that the Emperor found any
fault with the Marshal for the quietude which was the
direct consequence of his orders. But such evidence
as this can hardly add force to that which those orders
themselves afford. This myth of the day's operations
being affected by any fault of Ney's could, in short,
never have been originated, had the character of any
less person than Napoleon been at stake ; and, once
examined, it may be dismissed unhesitatingly to the
limbo of exploded Waterloo legends. In expecting
the English to stand at Quatre Bras alone, until he
should come in upon their flank, and that whilst such
keen eyes as those of Wellington and Müffling were Sib. i. 251.
Supp.
watching the open country between Bry and Quatre Disp. x.
527.
Bras, Napoleon appears as vainly sanguine, on this
side, as in his notion that the Prussians had gone
off to Namur.

Before leaving this important letter, it is right to
notice the expression in it, ' If D'Erlon had executed
the movement on St. Amand which the Emperor had
ordered, the Prussian army would have been totally

destroyed.'   Not that it is necessary to suppose this confirmatory of a fiction of Thiers, exposed in the last chapter, or contradictory to Napoleon's positive denial of his ordering D'Erlon's direct flank march unknown to Ney.   Hooper has well pointed out that this expression, which he has quoted alone, may fairly be conjectured to be merely a reference to Ney's repeated orders to detach troops from Quatre Bras as soon as he had beaten Wellington.   But in fact the matter is beyond conjecture, *if the first part of the paragraph be read together with the words quoted.*   This part applies the latter in the distinctest way to the action at Quatre Bras as the key, for it runs, ' If the corps of D'Erlon and Reille had been kept together, not an Englishman would have escaped of the corps which attacked you : ' so that to suppose D'Erlon detached on St. Amand *before the English were beaten*, would clearly be to make one part of the paragraph contradict the other.

Ante, p. 125.

Ante, p. 126. Hooper, p. 139.

Of the march of Blücher's army there is little to be added to what has been given in our brief narrative.   That Bülow, with his unbeaten corps, should have been posted to cover the rest of the army from any approach of the French by Mont St. Guibert, was a natural arrangement under the circumstances.   On the other hand, it was intended to put him at the head of the troops about to act at Waterloo next day ; and in this view his being encamped at Dion-le-Mont was an undoubted mistake, as it left him furthest of the Prussians from the desired point, and involved some

See ante, p. 136.

hours of delay in the important flank march of the
18th. That there was this unnecessary delay, owing
to the want of agreement between the disposition of
the corps for the night and their orders for the morning, has not escaped the notice of the chief German Claus.
p. 127.
critic, and we need add little to what he has said
hereon, which we shall have to refer to again. See p. 166.

It may seem at first less easy to excuse Blücher's
Staff for the want of information as to their doings,
which left Wellington exposed in an apparently isolated
position on the morning of the 17th. Müffling admits Mü. Mem.
p. 240.
that the Duke for a moment thought himself deceived,
when he at last heard from Zieten of the retreat begun See ante,
p. 188.
many hours before. Yet it was known to the former,
as appears from his narrative, that a Prussian officer,
on his way with some message at dark on the 16th, was
shot down by the French near Quatre Bras ; although
whether the message that thus miscarried was a sufficient announcement of the retreat has been doubted. Mü. Mem.
p. 238.
' The whole affair,' in Müffling's words, ' was somewhat
confused, and was never cleared up.' That it was so,
however, is chargeable mainly to himself, as the circumstances once known clearly show. For Major
Winterfeldt, riding up to Quatre Bras with his escort
to give Blücher's warning, was shot down by the Mil.
Woch. for
1869,
p. 709.
French skirmishers on the chaussée near Piermont,
and lay some time between their fire and that of
the Nassauers until the latter rescued him. Of an
officer who came to assist him he begged only that
his condition might be made known to the nearest

general of rank; for he thought it improper, even in his wounded state, to make known such alarming news as that he was charged with to a subordinate. No such person as he asked for could he get near him; and hence, though Müffling heard about dark in the Duke's presence (as he tells us) of the aide-de-camp's wound, no word came of what his message was, and it was probably thought to be of small importance. For this mistake, however, we may censure Müffling himself, or possibly the stiffness of character which first took Major Winterfeldt unnecessarily near the line of French skirmishers, and, when wounded by his own temerity, made him keep the message close. Neither Blücher nor Gneisenau—now that the truth is made clear—can any longer be charged with the supposed neglect to let their Ally know that the battle had gone against them; though it is fair to add that some additional precautions might well have been adopted by the latter, after he had taken command, and the fighting had come to an end, to acquaint the English general with the actual condition of affairs at so vital a point in the campaign.

The nature of the country enabling the quiescence of the French on both fields to be observed from the Duke's post, was sufficient reason for the rest he gave his troops before the retreat began. According to Müffling, he expected that this would involve severe fighting for the rearguard: but Müffling's experience of Napoleon's later manner of warfare enabled him to pronounce that the French, after bivouacking at dark,

Ante, p. 138.

Mü. Mem. p. 240.

would not break up before 10 a.m. ; and the result justified his prophecy. In the Wellington Memoran- Supp. Disp. x. 527. dum of 1862 the illustrious writer infers that the pause of the French was owing to his own success at Quatre Bras the day before, and mentions nothing of any apprehension of his being pressed. But this portion of the Memorandum is far from accurate, erring so widely as to put the advance of the French against his left at between 3 and 4 p.m., and it can hardly be accepted as being so authentic as the Memoirs* of his German attendant, who wrote upon the campaign with all the freshness of a mind charged with recent events.

Wellington's movement from Quatre Bras, the perfect way in which his strong cavalry and a single division of infantry masked the retreat of the rest, and the complete order in which he carried off so large and miscellaneous a force from before the face of the most renowned general of the world handling superior numbers, cannot be passed over in our comments. It attracted deserved admiration at the time from foreign Report of Gen. observers, though its details must be studied in the Alava to Spanish work of his friendly English critic, Kennedy, who was Government, employed in conducting it, to understand their perfec- Doc. 105. tion. Deliberation in movement is hardly (as certain Kenn, p. 17, 18. admiring commentators on the preceding events be- See for example, lieve) the perfection of a general's qualities. But the Hooper, p. 81. deliberation of the morning of the 17th had a special

* Müffling's Memoirs, though by his desire not published until after his decease, bear the unmistakable impress of being written (for this portion) not later than 1818–19, probably from the same notes which served for his early history of the campaign.

object, and was justified by the reasons already stated. For the rest, there is nothing in the day's work of Wellington on which it is necessary to enlarge further. The crown of the wise strategy which bade him halt to fight at Waterloo was yet to be won. The next day would show whether the mutual confidence of the Allies, and their unshaken resolve to join as soon as possible in a decisive blow, were to redeem the errors made at the outset of the campaign.

We have seen that Napoleon, as late as noon, was in complete ignorance of the fresh combination on which his enemies were bent. When he did at length give Grouchy positive orders, they were for a point

See Map.

which threw him (as a glance at the Map will show) to the east of and outside the line which the Prussians had taken, and left him at night much farther from Waterloo than they. These orders too were not given until midday, and the verbal one not very long before. The

Thi. xx.
153, 154.

letter indeed, according to Thiers, was delivered before 11 a.m. ; but the same historian says* that Napoleon,

Ante,
p. 142.
Cha.p.206.

on despatching it, galloped off from Bry to Marbais, a ride of less than two miles, and thence sent his second letter to Ney, dated ' at noon.' Grouchy has himself protested against the notion of his having obtained these instructions before noon, and his statement is

Ibid. Note.

exactly confirmed by that of Gérard, a witness in most

---

* It is at this point that Thiers attacks Grouchy's accuracy as to hours. If that Marshal has not always been accurate, he has, at least, a better excuse than the historian, who contradicts him here with one of his usual vague phrases, ' d'après les indications les plus certaines,' without naming any special authority whatever.

points unfavourable to him, who received his own order ' towards half-past twelve.' Charras and Quinet have exposed fully the mendacious deception of the ' Mémoires ' version, which, by omitting the hour of Grouchy's movement, and coupling its mention with the morning orders to Ney (falsely said to be given *à la pointe du jour*), is designed to impress the reader with the idea that Grouchy was sent off soon after daybreak, and wilfully halted long at Gembloux.　We need not, therefore, follow this matter further.　Those of their countrymen to whom the works of these critics are accessible have no longer an excuse for being blinded on this head.　Even Thiers has not attempted here to follow the imperial author whose veracity he commends.　His own version would but put Napoleon's order an hour earlier than the admitted time, making, on so wretchedly wet an evening as that which followed, no practical difference in the position taken up at Gembloux.　It must be noted here, that, among the charges heaped by the ' Mémoires ' upon Grouchy, is that of having only made *two leagues* that afternoon ; but, in fact, the distance from the village of St. Amand, where part of Vandamme's corps lay, to the quarters they occupied that night on the north side of Gembloux, was really more than eight miles, and the march was made in heavy rain through a narrow lane, as before mentioned.

Thiers, in describing the movement, has raised against the Marshal three distinct charges of his own, abandoning those of the ' Mémoires ' to oblivion.

Cha. 205.
Quin.
p. 165.
Mém. ix.
94.

Mém. ix.
100.

Belg. Gov.
Survey.

Ante,
p. 143.

Thi. xx.
173.

Having assumed beforehand that Grouchy 'lacked
entirely the sagacity required in an officer of advance-
guard charged with the look-out of an army,' he
blames him, first for not, on receiving his verbal orders,
having pushed a reconnaissance to his left on the road
followed by the Prussians of Zieten and Pirch, nor
even any to Gembloux; secondly, for galloping off
'very inconsiderately, like a feather-pated fellow'
[*comme une tête légère*], towards Namur; and lastly,
for allowing his infantry to stay too long on the Ligny
ground before marching. Only those who discern
the final purpose of these attacks would understand
the importance the historian attaches to them, thrown
as they are into his narrative with a light dexterity
which hides the appearance of the writer's art. That
purpose is best shown by the introductory sentence of
this part of the narrative, which we quote entire as the
Thi. xx.   pith of the argument : ' Three cavalry reconnaissances,
172.   one on Namur, two on Wavre [by the roads of Tilly
and Gembloux, just spoken of], would have in a few
hours found out what was going on ; and Grouchy,
whom Napoleon had left at 11 a.m., might have known
the truth at 3 or 4 p.m., and between 4 and 9 have
got very close to Wavre, or to the left of the Dyle, if
he chose to cross that stream, and put himself into
the closest possible communication with Napoleon.'
Neither this statement, nor the particular allegations
which it preludes, can at all bear the test of comparison with admitted facts. Let us look at these a
little closely.

Napoleon left Grouchy, with his verbal orders, and went straight to Marbais. From Marbais to Tilly is less than a mile, and Napoleon had with him three divisions of cavalry. If it was right to send horse ^{Thi. xx.} along the country roads beyond Tilly (and who can now doubt that it was so ?) the duty would plainly be Napoleon's own, who was between Grouchy and these roads, and was about, in moving to Quatre Bras, to leave them closer to his right than Grouchy to his left. Plainly, they were not reconnoitred because the Emperor did not in the least suspect the truth, that they formed the line to be pursued ; not from any diffi-culty, or from any notion that Grouchy, who had been left behind and farther away from them, would sup-ply this omission, made in the same careless confidence ^{Letter to} which assumed the whole Prussian army to be ' *mise* ^{Ney, ante,
pp. 139,} *en déroute.*' As to the reconnoitring of the Gembloux ^{140.} road, the well-known report of General Berton, who ^{Quoted} was one of the cavalry commanders detached early ^{from a
Précis by} by Napoleon, shows that this had been done at 9 a.m., ^{Berton.
Loben S.} and that Prussians had been found near that place. It ^{p. 228,
and Cha.} could have been of no use for Grouchy to report what ^{p. 192.} was already known. His proceeding on first taking his command, and whilst awaiting the defiling of his infantry out of Ligny and St. Amand, to inquire personally as to the truth of the reports sent up by Pajol from the Namur road, so far from being ' incon-siderate,' was so obvious a necessity, in the absence of definite orders, that had all gone well with the French it might have been used to prove the sagacity of

Grouchy and that of the Emperor, who selected an officer so suited for this particular duty.   The charge as to the needless delay of the infantry is directly

Ante,
p. 143.

disproved by Gérard's narrative, already referred to, which Thiers has elsewhere not omitted to use. That distinguished officer, whose testimony leans, where there is any doubt, against Grouchy, declares

See Orig.
in Cha. p.
193, 206.

that he ' kept close to Vandamme, for whom he had to wait, and the troops arrived as soon as was humanly possible in the torrents of rain and over frightful roads.'

The evidence, however, which completely absolves Grouchy from any charges of error in delay, and which renders a more detailed disproof of these almost super-fluous, lies in the simple words of his written orders :

See Orig.
in Cha.
p. 192.

' Move to Gembloux.   You will reconnoitre the roads to Namur and Maestricht, and will follow up the enemy.'   Grouchy's conduct, his position that even-

Ante,
p. 144.

ing, and his occupation by cavalry of Perwez and Sart-les-Walhain, were the exact performance of these orders.   The weather, and the hour at which they were received, must bear the rest of the responsibility. It was not Grouchy who put the movement off until the fine half of the summer day was spent.   It was not Grouchy who sent Grouchy to Gembloux instead of through Tilly toward Wavre, or across the Dyle.   It was not Grouchy who ordered reconnaissances to the east, and none to the west in the space between him and his main army.

In our narrative we have made no mention of any

further instructions sent to the Marshal that day.
Historians of many nations—historians who have no As Brial. ii. 409.
national predilections to indulge—have been led astray
by the positive assertions of the two St. Helena narra- Gourg. p. 70.
tives, that an order and its duplicate were sent to
Grouchy during the night, at an interval of four hours, Mém. ix. 102.
acquainting him with the coming battle, and instruct-
ing him how best to co-operate. The second version
even goes so far as to name the number of men which
Grouchy was to detach towards the Emperor's right !
If these tales have passed with critics of other nations,
we can hardly blame Thiers for admitting them into Thi. xx. 179.
his history, in the teeth of the exposure of their falsity Cha.p.329.
by Charras. As Quinet has written later than either,
however, we may quote what he says, to which we believe it would be difficult to add weight by a word of
our own : ' The two officers sent by Napoleon were Quin. p. 182.
never seen by Grouchy. No one has ever been able to
give their names. The orders they are asserted to
have carried are not to be found registered in the Staff
records. What is still more to the purpose, in the dispatches which followed, Napoleon made no mention
whatever of these orders of the night. He does not
insist upon their execution. He does not even refer
to them, contrary to invariable custom.' In brief,
they are manifest inventions.

Summary.

To resume the events of the 17th. Napoleon in
the morning believed the Prussians retreating in

disorder on Namur and Liège, and, though intending
now to turn against the English, thought it undesirable
to push his tired troops this day beyond Quatre Bras.
He directed Ney, therefore, to seize that post, if only
held by a rearguard ; but should the English army
stand there, he himself would, on its being reported,
move against their flank to crush them.   It was near
noon before he took any decided step, by moving
Lobau on to the Quatre Bras road, and by giving
Grouchy charge of 33,000 men, with verbal orders to
follow the Prussians.   Before this hour the Prussians
were collecting at Wavre, and were perfectly secure
from any molestation for to-day.   Before this hour,
Wellington had begun an orderly retreat on Waterloo,
where he wished to fight a defensive action ; so that
Napoleon's own advance against the English, and
positive orders to Ney at noon to do the same, were
too late to entangle even the rearguard.   When leaving
for Quatre Bras, resolved at last to follow Wellington
up, Napoleon ordered Grouchy to march on Gembloux ; but he quite omitted to reconnoitre the roads
between the Marshal's line and his own, by which the
whole of Zieten and Pirch's corps had gone to Wavre.
Grouchy only at 2 a.m. on the 18th had made up his
mind to march after daylight that morning in the direction of Wavre, having been much confused by the reports of the evening before, but believing some of the
Prussians, at any rate, were endeavouring to keep near
Wellington.   Wellington, before deciding to fight on
his chosen ground next day, had had the full assurance

of hearty co-operation from Blücher. He had brought together about 68,000 men only, but had 18,000 more of his field army on detachment ten miles to his right, and 90,000 Prussians (at the lowest estimate of Blücher's force) as near to his left ; whilst Napoleon's fighting strength was reduced (after deducting losses and Girard's division, left at Ligny) to 72,000 men ; and his only possible aid was from Grouchy's 33,000 men, who were all but double* the distance from him that Blücher's army was, and this owing to his own orders. He was in ignorance of the Prussian doings and designs. There is not a tittle of evidence to confirm, and every reason to disbelieve, his story that he sent fresh orders that night to Grouchy. Weighing all these facts fairly, it appears the inevitable deduction that the Allies had now thoroughly out-manœuvred their enemy, and that their better strategy and his own mistakes during the day had placed him at a fearful disadvantage in the struggle of the morrow.

* Full fourteen miles as the crow flies—the Prussians not more than eight.

LECTURE VI.

EVENTS OF THE 18TH.—COMMENTS.—SUMMARY.

THE early daylight showed Napoleon the army of his adversary motionless in its position. The English had passed the rainy night in much discomfort; but his own soldiers, almost destitute of firewood, had suffered still more from the downpour of rain, which only ceased at about 4 a.m. On the report of his artillery officers, that the ground would require some hours before the guns could move on the muddy fields, Napoleon delayed the preparations for the battle, though his troops were put under arms at an early hour. He expressed his satisfaction at the firm countenance of the English, discussed his intended manœuvres, and counted up confidently his chances of success. He had in his whole air and bearing the manner of one who scented a coming triumph, and felt no touch of fear of such an unexpected disaster as might follow the arrival of a fresh army on his flank. No allusion is mentioned, even in his own narratives, as made by him that morning, to any possible aid from Grouchy, nor any sign that he thought the Prussians near. After receiving a report from

Cha.p.210.

Mem. ix. 114.
Gourg. p. 72.
Thi. xx. 181 and 188.

his chief engineer, General Haxo, that no signs of intrenchments were to be seen in the enemy's position, he dictated his orders for the battle, and proceeded soon after 8 a.m. to marshal his troops in array in three grand lines, in the most deliberate manner, upon the slope opposite the position of Wellington. We need not give the particulars of this parade, which nearly all writers have taken directly from his own glowing description, revealing at its close the real purpose of this display : ' The spectacle was magnificent ; and the enemy, who was so placed as to behold it down to the last man, must have been struck by it ; the army must have seemed to him double in number what it really was.' There is no doubt that he sought to affect beforehand the spirits of the unsounder portion of the motley army opposed to him ; as he strove, at the same time, to raise those of his own soldiers, by making a personal inspection of them corps by corps, and appealing to their enthusiasm. Wellington, in his quieter fashion, was as active as his antagonist. His troops had also been under arms as soon as their enemy, and his staff from the earliest hour busy in placing each brigade in its assigned position, so as to give full weight to the value of the whole, and check the enemy effectually until Blücher's promised aid should arrive.

Mém. ix. 111, 112.

Sib. i. 327.

The communication between the Allies was unbroken. Whilst Wellington made an early survey of his line of defence, General Müffling was engaged in preparing a proposal for the co-operation

Mü Mem.
p. 242.
Mü. Hist.
p. 17.
of the Prussians, so as to use it with the greatest effect.

This scheme provided for each of the three probable cases of the day in the following manner :—

(1.) *Should the enemy attack Wellington's right*, the See Map. Prussians were to march upon Ohain, a point beyond his left, and on the shortest road to it from Wavre ; thus arriving without interruption, and supporting him with a reserve equal to the whole force attacking, and able to act freely on the open ground before Waterloo, as required.

(2.) *Should he attack Wellington's centre or left*, Ibid. and Prussian corps was to march by St. Lambert one Lasne, and take the French on the right flank, whilst another body by Ohain supported the English.

(3.) *Should the enemy* (instead of pressing the English) *march on St. Lambert*, the key-point of the country between Wavre and Waterloo, thus threatening to separate the Allies, then the Prussians would stand there to receive him in front, whilst Wellington, advancing direct from Waterloo, would take him in flank and rear.

At half-past 11, Napoleon was seen moving to an attack, seemingly directed against the centre ; and word was sent forthwith to Blücher that *the second case was occurring*, and that the Prussians were to Comp. Mü.
Hist. 17,
18, and
Pr. Off.
58, 75. act accordingly. Müffling had just now heard from Wavre that Bülow led the advance, and he charged his aide-de-camp to show that general his letter to

Blücher : but the Marshal himself was in front, and proceeded forthwith to take the needful steps.

Long before Napoleon went into battle he had evidently had some account of Zieten's movement on Wavre, and received Grouchy's two night reports from Gembloux, already mentioned. It must have been to the last of these, the missing one, that he replied in his morning instructions, dated 10 a.m. : 'You only speak of two Prussian columns which have passed through Sauvenière and Sart-les-Walhain. [In Grouchy's first letter *he spoke of three columns, and mentioned other places*.] Yet reports inform me of a third of some strength, going by Gentinnes on Wavre. The Emperor is about to attack the English, who have taken up position at Waterloo. Therefore His Majesty desires you to direct your movements upon Wavre, in order to come near to us, and connect yourself with our operations, pushing before you the Prussian corps which have taken this direction, and which may have stopped at Wavre, *where you are to arrive as soon as possible*. Follow up the enemy who have just gone to your right, by some light corps, to observe their movements and pick up stragglers. Do not omit to keep up your communication with us.' Thus Napoleon, though now made aware that some of the retreating Prussians had moved in a line parallel to his own, still looked on these as a mere detachment, and clung to the delusion that a great part at least of Blücher's troops had separated from them and gone eastward.

Ante, p. 144.

See Orig. in Cha. p. 226, or Claus. p. 147. See ante, p. 144.

Far from any such guess were the realities of the
hour.   Round Wavre that morning nearly 100,000 of
his enemies were preparing to join in the coming battle.
The country between Wavre and the field of Waterloo
resembles in its character certain well-known parts of
Devonshire, being broken into rounded hills, with
patches of wood upon their slopes, and traversed by
Pers. Obs. lanes deep and miry in the hollows.   The chief cross-
road is that which passes over the highest of the hills
(on which stands the conspicuous Church of St. Lam-
See Map. bert), falls steeply down into the valley of the Lasne,
at a village of the same name, and, ascending again to
Plancenoit, leads on to the Brussels and Charleroi road
near to the farm of Caillou, where Napoleon's headquarters were established on the night of the 17th.
A similar road, more to the north, conducts more
directly by Froidmont and Ohain on to the crest which
formed the front of the English position.   On both of
these the Prussians had started early to take their
share in the battle.   Bülow was to lead, followed by
Claus.
p. 126.
Pr. Off.
p. 58. Pirch, along the former road; Zieten to take the line to
Ohain.   Thielemann was ordered to act as rearguard
and cover the movement, and, in case of no enemy
appearing at Wavre, to follow finally on Plancenoit.
Ante,
p. 150. But Bülow, it will be remembered, was some miles on
the wrong side of Wavre, and his first brigade had
hardly got clear of the town, when a fire, breaking
out in the narrow street through which his corps
defiled, stopped the rest of the troops for nearly two
hours.   A further delay arose from the passage of

Zieten's corps on their way to the northern road, Claus. p. 156. Pr. Off. p. 8.
crossing that to St. Lambert, occupied by the other
column. Moreover, the troops, drenched and tired
the night before, were not originally started until Clausewitz here (who was present).
7 a.m. So considerable were the delays from these
causes, added to the wretched nature of the roads,
that it was 3 p.m. before the tail of Bülow's column
reached St. Lambert, although his leading brigade had
been there before noon. It was plain, therefore, that Pr. Off. p. 58 and 75.
the Prussians could take no share in the early part of
the great battle, and that Wellington must bear the
full brunt until the afternoon wore some hours on.

Grouchy had moved no earlier than they. Not- Thi. xx. 255. Cha.p.296.
withstanding his orders directing Vandamme to start
at 6 a.m., and Gérard at 7, there was some delay in
moving off the troops, and each corps left its quarters
near Gembloux from one to two hours later than the
appointed time. Their march was also slow; for it
was made on a single indifferent country road, and in
very close order—the hindmost corps (Gérard's) being
of course frequently obliged to halt. It was passing
Sart-les-Walhain at half-past 11, where Grouchy, with
his chief generals, had paused for a repast, when sud- Thi. xx. 255. Cha.p.296.
denly a deep and constant rolling from the left told
the practised ears that listened, that Napoleon was
engaged in another general action. Although the
letter of 10 a.m. from Waterloo was not yet received,
there was no doubt in Grouchy's mind, or that of any
other listener, that the Emperor had come upon and
engaged the English army. Then arose the natural

discussion as to which way the present march should
be continued.   It will be remembered that the morning orders to the commanders of corps were only for a
Ante, pp.
144, 145. movement on Sart-les-Walhain, with a mere reference
to the possibility of its being prolonged beyond that
place. Information obtained there by Grouchy, before
Thi. xx.
256. the troops came up, had told him that the bulk of the
Cha.p.297. Prussians had really reached Wavre, and caused him
to order the march to continue at once on that town,
Ibid. reporting his proceeding thither to Napoleon.   The
road would lie naturally through the villages of Nil
See Map. St. Vincent, Corbaix, and Baraque ; and, in effect, the
head of Vandamme's column (which Exelmans with
his cavalry preceded) had reached the former of these
Cha.p.298.
Thi. xx.
251. places when the firing was heard. Should the army
then wheel to its left, making straight from Corbaix to
the bridges known to be upon the Dyle at Mousty and
Ottignies, and there passing the river, hurry towards
Plancenoit, where it was guessed Napoleon would be
found ?   Or should the march be continued to Wavre,
where Grouchy believed his duty to lie, inasmuch as
the Prussians were his mark, and the Prussians were
last heard of there ?   Gérard with much warmth urged
the former view, and made light of the supposed difficulty of carrying across the guns, which was raised by
Grouchy's general of artillery. This indeed his chief
engineer, siding with Gérard, undertook to remove.
The Marshal, however, decided against this suggestion.
The arrival of his troops, as he judged, over the
fourteen miles of difficult ground, and with an un-

certain river-passage to make, could not be counted on
to be of service to Napoleon that day ; and his own Here chiefly Charras, who writes from Grouchy's narrative.
business was to press the Prussians, who might as
possibly be facing him at Wavre, or retiring by a line
of their own on Louvain, as moving on Waterloo
according to the supposition of Gérard. Again, if
they should discover the proposed march, and fall
upon Grouchy's right flank, which would be exposed
to them during the whole movement, the consequences
might be disastrous to the Emperor's plan, which supposed him to be pursuing them, and not turning aside
to follow a course of his own. In spite of warm
remonstrances, the march on Wavre was continued,
and a little before 2 p.m. Vandamme's infantry, pre-
ceded by Exelmans' horse, reached Baraque, two Thi. xx. 264. Cha.p.304.
miles south from the town, and became engaged soon
after with a considerable force of Prussians—the rearguard in fact of Pirch, who with half his corps had
started on to follow Bülow to St. Lambert, leaving Pr. Off. p. 59.
Major-General Brause to cover his movement with the
rest. These had been flanked on the side of Mont St.
Guibert by a detachment left by Bülow to guard the
defile there made by one of the heads of the Dyle ;
and this detachment, under a Colonel Ledebur, had
held its post until the advance of Exelmans all but
cut it off from the rest of the Prussians. With some
difficulty Ledebur joined Brause, who then, at half-
past 2, gave the signal for retreat, and crossing the
Dyle at Bierge, broke the bridge, and pressed on to
overtake the rest of the corps, leaving a single regiment Ibid.

of hussars and two battalions of infantry to guard the
Ante,
p. 166.
part of the stream he was quitting.   Before this time
Zieten's corps was now, after some delay, on the way
towards Ohain, and the rear divisions of Bülow near
St. Lambert.   Thielemann only, with the 3rd Corps,
Claus. p.
134 and
Pr. Off.
p. 59.
was left at Wavre, by 3 p.m. ; and he was just preparing to file off in the direction laid down in his
orders (which would have carried him slightly to the
left of St. Lambert by a separate cross-road), when the
approach of Vandamme close to the town compelled
him to halt to defend the passage of the river.   Six
battalions of the corps had already gone on, and
Thielemann, who reckoned the enemy at no more than
the 10,000 to 12,000 men whom he could see deploy-
Pr. Off.
p. 86, 87.
ing, declined or omitted to recall them, thus remaining
himself at Wavre with 15,200 soldiers, all told.   At
Pr. Off.
p. 87.
Thi. xx.
266.
Cha.p.306.
about 4 p.m., whilst Grouchy was arranging for the
attack, he received (the messenger having gone round
by Quatre Bras and Gembloux) his first communication from Napoleon since his march began.   This was
the letter of 10 a.m. of the 18th already given, which
Ante,
p. 165.
distinctly informed him that the Emperor was about
to fight the English at Waterloo, and ordered him to
‘ direct his movements on Wavre,’ ‘ where he was to
arrive as soon as possible.’   Naturally enough, the
Marshal concluded his noonday choice to be the correct one, and himself in the right place.   He proceeded,
therefore, to the attack of Thielemann, in which we
leave him engaged for the present, whilst we return
once more to follow the fortunes of his master.

It is not within our allotted task to trace the details of the tremendous contest in which the Emperor was engaged. Those who would view it completely analysed, and understand how distinct were the five great phases into which Napoleon broke it by separate attacks, should study the work of Sir J. Shaw Kennedy, in which this subject is treated with a clearness no other writer has reached. The tactical skill and energy with which Wellington handled his motley force had never, we believe, been done full justice to before. He held his ground for some hours at least without direct help, against an army which this writer—a careful eye-witness—insists should not, allowing for the inferior *morale* of the bulk of the Allies, be estimated at a less disproportion than seven* to four. That he thus held it was due, as Kennedy proves, not less to his own special ability than to the only two other causes to which the success of his resistance has been assigned, the tenacity of the British infantry, and the arrival of Prussian succour. It is the last of these which we have more particularly to examine the weight of, in order to judge the relation of the strategy to the tactics of the day. Kenn. p. 57. Ibid. p. 127.

We left Blücher at St. Lambert at the head of his left column, and communicating with Müffling. Half of Bülow's corps only was up† some time after Ante, p. 164, and Pr. Off. p. 75.

* Or six to four if Lobau be deducted from Napoleon's] strength. Kennedy estimates that of Wellington as worth only 41,000 fighting men. This, however, is but a personal opinion of that writer's.

† The exact time of this assembly of the half corps is not on

midday, and Blücher had at first resolved to wait
for more men until he could fall with concentrated
strength on the right flank of the enemy, which his
reconnoitring officer told him was open and unguarded.
Lest the movement should be discovered and inter-
Pr. Off.
p. 75.
cepted in the steep valley of the Lasne which lay below
him, he resolved to seize the other side of it, on which
was much wood. Bülow, with the two divisions
in hand and the cavalry of the corps, pressed on
accordingly, crossed the brook without opposition,
and gained the edge of the plateau beyond, which
stretches away towards Plancenoit and the Brussels
road beyond, along which the French had come.
Then Blücher, impatient at the delays in rear, and at
the heat of the firing which he had now approached,
determined to attack at once with the troops in hand,
and ordered Bülow to deploy accordingly. The passage of the valley by miry lanes had been slow in
spite of much exertion, and the deployment was made
under similar difficulties. Thus it was half-past 4
before the two divisions, covered by their horse, were
ready for the advance on the French right.

Thi. xx.
196.
Let us turn to watch Napoleon during the five
hours already spent. He had begun his battle with
cannonade, followed at noon by an attack on Hougoumont made by Reille's corps, and then directed a more
serious onslaught at half-past 1 on the English left
Ibid. 200.
centre with the almost intact corps of D'Erlon. Before

record; but Bülow's leading division reached St. Lambert before
noon, and the last of the four not until 3 p.m. See ante, p. 167.

this last took place, however, there had been seen on the hill of St. Lambert a body of troops, of strength and nation unknown, but which could only be part of Grouchy's force, or some detachment of Prussians. Napoleon could not have attached any serious importance to this apparition at first, since he made no effort to stop the strange corps, beyond sending to his right two divisions of light cavalry amounting to 2,400 sabres. He was not long in ignorance. A Prussian non-commissioned officer of hussars was taken and brought in with a letter from Bülow, announcing his arrival at St. Lambert, and requesting Wellington's instructions ; for this messenger had left before Müffling's despatch, sent for their guidance, could have been delivered to the Prussian staff. On hearing the alarming intelligence that 30,000 Prussians were approaching his flank, the Emperor moved Lobau's two* remaining infantry divisions to support the cavalry, thus detaching a force of 10,000 men, while turning to press his own battle forward with the rest of his troops.

Thi. xx. 200. Cha.p.225.

Thi. xx. 201. Cha.p.227.

Ante, p. 166.

Before this prisoner was taken, Napoleon had felt (probably after the first appearance at St. Lambert) some doubts as to whether his own orders to Grouchy had been precise enough. He had heard nothing further from the Marshal, and could only refer again to the night reports received from him, when he dictated the following dispatch, with a postscript added after the capture of the hussar :

* It must be remembered one of Lobau's three was with Grouchy.

See Orig.
Cha.p.228.
or Claus.
p. 148.

'The Field of Waterloo, June 18, 1 p.m.

'You have written this morning at two o'clock, that you would march on Sart-les-Walhain ; therefore (donc) your design is to move on Corbaix, or Wavre. This movement is conformable to His Majesty's arrangements, which have been made known to you. However, the Emperor orders me to tell you that you should constantly manœuvre in our direction. It is for you to see where we are, and to regulate yourself accordingly, so as to connect our communications, and to be always prepared to fall upon any of the enemy's troops which may endeavour to annoy our right, and crush them.

'At this instant, battle is engaged on the line before Waterloo. The enemy's centre is at Mont Saint-Jean. Manœuvre therefore to join our right.

'P.S.—A letter, which has just been intercepted, tells that General Bülow is about to attack our flank ; we believe we see this corps on the heights of St. Lambert. So lose not an instant in drawing near and joining us, in order to crush Bülow, whom you will catch in the very act (en flagrant délit).'

Thi. xx.
270.
Cha.p.307,
or Original
Report,
Doc. 153.

This letter reached Grouchy indeed, but not until near 6 p.m. at the earliest (or 7 p.m. by his own statement), when he was thoroughly committed to a severe action at Wavre. It was too late then to attempt to join the Emperor that day, and the unfortunate Marshal was obliged to content himself with the hope that Napoleon might have triumphed without him.

The letter appears to have been dispatched as Ante, p. 172.
D'Erlon's grand attack was formed. This, repulsed
with heavy loss, was followed by a third attempt, not
less fruitless, made by the cavalry upon the English
centre. The fourth phase of the battle was more hope-
ful for the French; for Ney's infantry, about 6 p.m.,
renewing the assault on the left centre, carried
the post of La Haye Sainte, threw skirmishers and Kenn. p. 122.
guns beyond, and forced a gap in the British centre,
the two brigades defending this part being so thinned
that they could no longer keep their position.* Wellington's personal coolness and energy enabled him to
repair the breach with his Brunswick and Nassau Ibid. p. 127.
troops, and by his exertions and those of his remaining Staff the peril was overcome: for Napoleon, not
aware apparently of the advantage his troops had
gained, did not follow it up by using his reserve. By
7 p.m. the danger had died away.

Long before this hour Napoleon's attention had
been seriously drawn to his own threatened right.
Bülow had advanced, as we have seen, with half his Ante, p. 172.
corps, and soon forced back the light cavalry which
covered Lobau, and engaged the infantry of that
general. An hour later (at half-past 5) the whole Pr. Off. p. 76. Cha.p.251.
of the Prussian corps, 29,000 strong, was on the
ground; Lobau, after a brave resistance, was forced
back on Plancenoit, and the Prussian guns were
within range of the Brussels road. As Blücher was

---

* The narrative of Kennedy, who was the Staff officer of the
division thus forced, is here followed *literatim*.

pushing his attack, advices reached him from Thielemann, hard pressed by Grouchy's superior force ; but
the brave old man, willing rather to expose his own
Pr. Off.
p. 77. rear than to slacken his attack at the decisive point,
sent word to his lieutenant to hold his own as best
he could, since no reinforcement could at present be
spared him. So vigorously did he at the same time
advance on Plancenoit, that Napoleon, between 6 and
7 p.m., was forced to aid Lobau with a division of the
Guard 4,000 strong, and three of its batteries, which
Ibid. p. 78.
Thi. xx.
237.
Cha.p.252. for a time saved the village from being carried by
Bülow's men. It was about this time, be it remembered, that Wellington on his side arrested the attack
directed from La Haye Sainte on his centre.

Zieten meanwhile, by the same hour, had made his
way along the road through Ohain ; and his leading
division, under Steinmetz, followed by the cavalry of
the corps, approached the extreme left of Wellington,
which rested on the building called Papelotte. Their
mere appearance had the effect of strengthening the
British centre, for Vivian's and Vandeleur's brigades of
cavalry, bodies of horse almost intact, on Müffling's
Compare
Mü. Mem.
p. 247, and
Sib. ii. 149. suggestion (who was on that wing awaiting Zieten), or
prompted by the urgency of the case, moved off along
the rear to reinforce the weaker point. At this important crisis of the battle, Napoleon was preparing to
advance his last reserve of Guards, in hopes of forcing
the English from the field before the Prussian attack
was developed. Suddenly Zieten, misled by a recon-
Mü. Mem.
p. 248. noitring Staff officer who reported that the English

right was already retreating, recalled his advance and changed their direction, intending to march by his left towards the column of Bülow, and unite his attack with that which Blücher personally led. The inevitable delay which such withdrawal from the direct movement onwards would have caused was happily averted. Müffling galloped after the retiring division, explained that the staff officer had, in his haste, made the dangerous error of mistaking the movements of wounded and stragglers to the rear for a retreat, and caused Zieten to turn back and press the advance on Papelotte. During the interval thus lost, the French right, Durutte's divisions of D'Erlon's corps, followed by Marcognet, had advanced with other troops to support the assault made on the English right centre by Napoleon's last reserve, the famed attack of the Guards. Durutte reached Papelotte and La Haye, an adjacent building, both held by Prince Bernard's Nassauers, and for a few minutes seemed effectually to divide Wellington's line from the coming aid. For a few minutes only, for Steinmetz's division, turned back at Müffling's request, suddenly appeared on their flank, and, by a charge made at about half-past 7,* cleared the disputed

Mü Mem. p. 248. Pr. Off. p. 79.

Cha.p.259. Thi. xx. 240.

Thi. xx. 242.

* There is a natural tendency here for English writers to make the attacks of Blücher's corps later, and Prussian earlier, than they really were. We fix this one of Zieten's, by the original report of Blücher (Doc. 93), which is very distinct. The Austrian Commissioner's narrative (which is highly favourable to the Prussians) would date it (Doc. 102) at 7 p.m.; the Dutch historian earlier. We may be pretty sure, however, that Gneisenau, writing for Blücher, would not put the time any later than it really was. This

Loben S. p. 293.

N

Bernard's
Letter.
Doc. 34.
Cha.p.259.
Loben S.
p. 300.
Kenn.
p. 148.
buildings, shooting down (so hot was their haste) some of the Nassauers whom they took for French, and creating an irresistible panic among their surprised enemies, which soon reached the centre, and added to that caused by the discomfiture of the Guards in their gallant but useless assault.

These, indeed, had been altogether too weak for the work put on them; for, before they advanced, Napoleon had been compelled, by Blücher's pressure Thi. xx.
241.
Cha.p.255. on Plancenoit, to detach three additional battalions to that village, and had placed three more to maintain his communication with Lobau, thus leaving only ten disposable. Of these the Emperor retained a small reserve of two or three at the foot of the slope which Ibid. and
Loben S.
p. 296, &c.
Leeke's
'52nd at
Waterloo,'
I. ch. v.
Kenn. p.
141, 142. his army held, and sent the rest to the attack. Formed in two columns, with an interval between, they advanced, these veterans, with the steadiness of troops long accustomed to wrest victory from doubtful battle. Undismayed by the appalling spectacle presented by the ground between La Haye Sainte and Hougoumont, strewn with the ruins of their shattered cavalry, they drew near the right centre of the British line. The fire on both sides had slackened Loben S.
p. 298.
Cha.p.259.
Thi. xx.
240, &c.
Kenn.
p. 142. for want of ammunition, and loud above the dropping shots was heard the war-cry with which the warriors of the Empire heralded their assaults. But the British Guard, though sorely weakened by the

report of his also clearly fixes the capture of Plancenoit as the *last* important incident of the day. Mr. Leeke (i. 45) makes the defeat of the Guards as late as 8 p.m.

enemy's artillery, met them steadfastly face to face as they crowned the hill which marked Wellington's position; while on their left Colborne, peerless among all the brave men who led Wellington's battalions, coolly formed in line the 52nd, and, without other prompting than that of his own genius for battle, advanced against their flank. Checked thus by an unexpected enemy in front (for the British Guard had lain concealed from them by the crest of the hill), and surprised by the attack of the 52nd, they recoiled down the slope in disastrous confusion : and this the vigorous pursuit of Colborne, supported by other troops of Clinton's division, by Vivian's and Vandeleur's horse, and by Chassé's Dutch-Belgians (brought up by that general about 4 p.m. from the extreme right of the line), soon turned into a complete rout, which spread rapidly to their reserve battalions and the few remaining troops left about Napoleon's centre. As Colborne followed up the Guard along the chaussée that divided the field into its eastern and western parts, he was crossed by the mass of fugitives flying before Zieten's advance from the right of the French, and the two wings of Napoleon's army became blended into a mass of fugitives. Hope then died away in the hardiest breasts, and Emperor, Staff, and army moved rearward in common flight, quickened by the ever-increasing roar of Blücher's guns as the Prussians pressed closer and closer upon the defenders of Plancenoit.

See his
letter,
Leeke, I.
100.

For a full
discussion
of this
episode
see p. 200,
&c.

Kenn. p.
145, 146.
MS.
Report of
Clinton to
Lord Hill,
dated 19th.
Loben S.
p. 298, 299.

Leeke, I.
61.
See also
Gawler's
'Crisis of
Waterloo,'
U. S.
Journal,
1833.

Loben S.
p. 300, 302.
Kenn.
p. 150.

N 2

Thi. xx.
242, &c.
Cha.p.255.
Kenn.
p. 150.
Meanwhile Lobau, who altogether had 16,000 men placed under him that day, held his own in the village manfully. Not even amid the burning ruins by the Danube, where he first won Napoleon's praise,[*] and saved the Grand Army from an earlier Waterloo, had his brave general shown a more undaunted courage. Honoured be the man who by his devotion not only gave to his falling chief that last desperate chance, but time for escape when it too was lost, and the Empire overthrown He kept his post with desperate sacrifice on his side, and not less loss to his Report of Blücher. Doc. xcii. fierce assailants, until some time after Zieten's attack, developed more at every instant, had decided the fate of the French right wing, and the mass of Napoleon's army was in retreat before the general advance of the British line, which Wellington, with the instinct of genius, had ordered on the instant when he saw the

Pelet's
Guerre de
1809, III.
329.
Schneida-
wind's
Krieg von
1809, I.
427.
* At the battle of Aspern the personal gallantry of General Mouton (Lobau's family name) saved the village of Essling, and covered the approach to the French bridges from the Archduke Charles's last and most dangerous attack. But for his cool daring and Masséna's devotion, the French would have lost their retreat into the island of Lobau, and have been taken or destroyed in the trap Napoleon's old antagonist had laid for them. Even then it needed six weeks of repose and the victory of Wagram to restore confidence to the soldiers and prestige to their chief. As for the Personal
informa-
tion
gathered
at Vienna
from
private
sources. conqueror of Aspern, jealousy of his renown and of the possible consequences of another victory, gave rise to a base intrigue, which deprived him, at the critical hour, of the support of part of the troops placed nominally under him; and he laid down the sword which his own brother's hands had turned aside from the foe. The war was brought to a close, inglorious for Austria; and the great struggle on the Danube's banks bequeathed little but the knowledge of Napoleon's fallibility, and the titles to Masséna and Mouton of Prince of Essling and Count Lobau.

enemy losing all power of resistance. Then Pirch Pr. Off. p. 82.
joined Bülow's left, formed his fresh battalions into
columns of attack, and cast the French out of their
last stronghold. This success laid open the great road
behind to the Prussian guns, the fire of which now Ibid. p. 83.
almost crossed the English front, turning the French
defeat into the most disastrous rout of a great army
which history records, a rout which the Allied cavalry
pressed on so hastily to complete, as at first to ex- Sib. i. 243.
change sabre cuts with each other in the coming darkness. The two Marshals had now but to arrange that
Blücher's troops should keep up the pursuit of the
mass of fugitives which was all that was left of the
Grand Army. Gneisenau in person pushed this on
with the indefatigable energy which Blücher's own For details see Ense, p. 446, 447.
earnestness had infused into every man who served
under him that afternoon, and some of Bülow's cavalry
occupied Gosselies before break of day. Napoleon, Pr. Off. p. 85.
flying all through the darkness from his enemies,
hurried on with an escort of twenty chance horsemen Thi. xx. 254.
that night to Philippeville, pausing only at Charleroi
to send Marshal Grouchy word of the disaster.

Unconscious of his master's desperate fortunes,
that officer continued his own battle until dark. This
action at Wavre has in it few features of special
interest, and took just that course which might have
been anticipated from the relative strength of the two
armies. Grouchy failed to carry the town in face of
the steady resistance of the Prussians ; but, as his
troops came up, he made use of his superior numbers,

So his
Report,
Doc. 153.

Claus. p.
134, 137.
(Clause-
witz was
chief of
Staff to
Thiele-
mann.)

and with some notion of stopping the movement on
Waterloo, extended his left along the Dyle as far as
Limal, two miles higher up.　This passage, held until
the afternoon by the rearguard of Zieten, was now
found unguarded, the Prussians having moved off to
follow their own corps.　The French therefore, some
of Gérard's men, established themselves without difficulty on the left bank of the river, and repulsed an
attack which Thielemann himself made on them after
dark, when he discovered that his line of defence was
thus turned.　Like Grouchy, he remained that night
in ignorance of the victory gained at Waterloo.

Comments.

Thiers, after labouring with vast ingenuity to prove
that the delays of the two preceding mornings were
due to no fault of Napoleon, undertakes the yet harder
task of showing that the Great Captain was not responsible for the time wasted on the fated day itself.
It is admitted on all hands that the Emperor could
have had but three reasons for delay ; his expecting
Grouchy to join him, his anxiety to let the soil
harden, or his desire to display his strength impres-

Ante,
p. 159.
Gourg.
p. 72.
Mém. ix.
107.

sively before striking.　Notwithstanding his myth
of the double night orders to the Marshal, Napoleon,
in his own narratives, fixes the delay decisively
upon the two latter, especially on the state of the
ground, which was beyond all question unfavourable
to the offensive.　Aware of this, Thiers confines
his excuse for the temporary inaction to two heads.

The first of these is directed to show that the Emperor could not possibly have divined the advance of Blücher unobserved by Grouchy, since ' such a thing was of all things the least supposable.' When a critic makes a dogmatic assertion of this kind respecting military events which actually occurred, it is surely enough reply to point out that the special business of the strategist is to conceive beforehand the possibility of such events. Napoleon boasts that he had previously weighed well the characters of his opponents. Such study was worthless to him if he used it so ill as not to divine in the remotest degree what they were about to do. As for the Prussians having escaped from Grouchy by what this historian terms ' the real phenomenon of the blindness ' of that Marshal, this is answered by the facts effectually enough to satisfy anyone but those deaf to the truth in matters that concern Napoleon. The Emperor himself delayed the pursuit for half the day after Ligny, himself selected Grouchy to conduct it, and himself gave him the detailed instructions which took him to Gembloux. Upon the Emperor rests the responsibility of the movement made too late and too wide for its intended purpose.

Thi. xx. 283.

Ibid. 282.

Vide ante, p. 160.

Drouot, the chivalric chief of artillery to the Guard, charged himself with the delay, according to an interesting note in the Thiers narrative. Drouot, no doubt, gave his master his opinion in favour of delay ; and since he was notoriously a conscientious man, it is probable enough he took much blame to

Thi. xx. 283-285. Note.

himself in after days for the result. But Napoleon
had also been bred an artilleryman, had served as an
artillery general, had made more use of guns under his
own eye than any commander that ever lived.   Moreover, he had in his hand what Drouot could not grasp,
the strings of the strategic combinations of the whole
theatre of war : and if in spite of these facts we should
persist in putting upon others the decision he made
to spend the later hours of the forenoon in parade,
it can only be said that we are contradicted alike by
plain evidence and by his own narratives, in which
he assumes the full responsibility of the delay, and
justifies it by what he believed to be good and sufficient
reasons.

Ante, pp.
162, 163.

Wellington had chosen his battle-ground deliberately with his back to the forest of Soignies, a wood
everywhere traversable by infantry, and with several
roads leading through it from the rear of the position.
Napoleon, revenging himself at St. Helena for his
defeat by criticising his adversaries, asserted that
this position was so badly chosen as to render retreat
from it impossible, which fact alone, twice that day,
prevented the English general from retiring ! The
latter part of this statement needs no comment to
those who know the story of the battle ; indeed,
modern French historians do not attempt to follow
the Emperor here. The propriety of fighting with
the back to such a wood as that of Soignies is another
matter, one apparently in this case of theory ; and
hence we cannot do better than quote a short note

Mém. x.
174.

upon it from Jomini's narrative, since that writer is
the admitted head of the great school of theorists
who admire Napoleon's genius :

' This is one of the gravest questions of the grand
tactics of battles. I have discussed it in my " Précis
of the Art of War," *and incline to the opinion of
Wellington against that of Napoleon.*'

Passing to the more independent school of German
critics, it is natural to turn to the pages of Clausewitz,
who, not content with giving his special testimony in
this instance in favour of Wellington, has made the
attempt, in his ' Art of War,' to treat systematically
the subject of the use of forests by armies. He de-
scribes at the opening of his chapter a partially traversable wood (such as is and was that of Soignies) as
the first case to be considered, and thus, after some
considerations, lays down his theory, the first words
of which American experience would no doubt have
caused him greatly to modify :

' Wooded districts cannot in any manner be used
advantageously for defensive actions, except when
they lie to the rear. In this case they conceal from
the enemy all that passes in the defender's rear,
and at the same time serve to cover and facilitate his
retreat.'

If there be any virtue therefore at all in theory,
it would appear that the weight of its evidence
is directly against the assertion of Napoleon, and
in favour of the practical view which Wellington
undoubtedly entertained. And Wellington, be it

Jom. *Note,*
196.

Clause-
witz, ' De
la Guerre,'
Paris, edit.
1851, pp.
430, 431.

remembered, had had more actual experience of the defensive than his adversary. But all this discussion as to the wood becomes of little moment if it be decided that he had another plan altogether for his Vide evidence of Col. Ziegler (son of the Gen.). Büd. p. 10. retreat, should his centre have been forced. And that this was the case appears from the testimony of General Ziegler, commandant at Namur in 1821, to whom Wellington, after his visit to the ground, declared as follows, illustrating his remarks as he spoke by a pencil sketch : ' The last hour of the battle was indeed a trying one to me. But I should not have retreated on the wood of Soignies, as Napoleon supposed, thinking I should fall back on Brussels and the sea, but should have taken the direction to my left, that is towards Wavre, which would have given me the substantial advantage of drawing near the Prussian Army.' As it would plainly have been impossible to carry off his right wing in the direction thus indicated, it must have been divided from him and made a distinct retreat westward. And this possibility gives the most proper Discussed further at p. 217, &c. solution ever offered of his obstinacy (to be noticed later) in retaining the troops at Hal, which would have proved of real service in forming a rallying-point for the force thus to be left separated under Lord Hill.

French writers point naturally enough to the delay of Grouchy on the morning of the 18th as one of the Ante, p. 167. elements in the disasters of the day. We have shown that he moved at least as early as the Prussians ; and the facts bring plainly into view that element of war so often ignored by the historian, the condition and will of the soldier.   Troops that have had a long day's march in mire and rain, and a rest imperfect for lack of shelter, cannot always be got to take their rough morning meal and start on a new movement as early as the general desires.   Clausewitz, who amid deep theory reverts constantly to the practical conditions and difficulties of the warfare he had witnessed, sheds a plainer light here than any other critic.   He points out that from the field of Ligny, by Gembloux to Wavre, is a march of more than twenty miles, and that the distance was accomplished by Grouchy in just twenty-four hours, *under very unfavourable conditions of road and weather*.   In their best days he finds that Napoleon's troops, under such circumstances, often did not make over ten miles.   Such conditions, he adds, reduce marching to a half, or even a third, of what is laid down in the closet as possible.   And hence he concludes that Grouchy is not to be reprehended for slowness of movement, albeit he might have possibly accelerated his march slightly, had he not kept the bulk of the troops in one column. Claus. p. 132.

We have already referred to the same critic's evidence as to the stoppage in the Prussian flank march arising from the crossing of the columns.   As an eye-witness, and as a fellow-countryman of the distinguished officers concerned, his reflections are entitled to peculiar credit.   There can be no doubt, as he has shown, that mistakes in detail were made, Ante, p. 167. Claus. p. 127, 128.

which led to delay. On the other hand, there are
few who will not agree with his remark upon the
march, that 'its general design, to support the English left with 20,000 men, and throw the other 70,000
upon Napoleon's right, could not have been more
simple, practical, and effective.' He has pointed out
that most of the morning's delay occurred before a
shot was fired, and adds an expression of his belief,
that, 'if Wellington had been heard engaged at 8 or
9 a.m., the Prussian advance-guard would have been
on the ground by 12 or 1 o'clock.' The credit given
to Blücher and his staff for the conception of the
march may be slightly marred by its incidents ; but
high honour must ever be due to the old Marshal
for the noble exertions which redeemed these in the
end. The gesture of fire that urged on the plodding
columns, the oft-repeated entreaty to his labouring
artillerymen, 'Lads, you won't let me break my
word !' ('*Kinder, ihr wollt doch nicht dass ich wort-
brüchig werden soll !*') are among the details that best
deserve to be graven on the history of the day.

Von Ense, p. 447.

There is no statement more distinct and positive
in the narrative of Thiers than that in which he asserts
that, at 2 a.m. on the 18th, Grouchy wrote to Napoleon that he had resolved to march on Wavre at daybreak ('*que définitivement il marcherait sur Wavre dès
la pointe du jour*'). Here, then, is a test of the care
and honesty with which the historian has used his
materials, for the letter referred to is the missing one,
which has never seen the light since the day of

Thi. xx. 189.

Waterloo, and the contents of which can only be made out from indirect proofs. Of these we have the two replies of Napoleon already quoted, written at 10 a.m. and 1 p.m. The first desires Grouchy to *direct his movements on Wavre*; the second quotes from the Marshal's letter the latter's words, ' You have written at 2 a.m. *that you would march on Sart-les-Walhain.*' In addition to these letters (which in a dozen different publications should have met the eye of Thiers) he must have had at least the opportunity of access to the Bureau of War at Paris, from which Charras drew his copies of the detailed orders to Vandamme, showing that the morning's march was not to be begun till 6 a.m., and then to Walhain only, with some indistinct notion of an advance beyond. Yet, with all this proof open to him, Thiers, desiring to show that Napoleon had good reason for expecting aid from Grouchy that day, makes for this poor purpose the doubly false assertion as to the hour and object of the morning's intended march which we have pointed to above. As to any needless delay in the time of the movement forward, the best evidence that Vandamme's orders were for an early hour enough is that that general could not manage to march till 7 a.m., evidence sufficient of the wisdom of Clausewitz's remarks on this portion of the campaign.

Ante. p. 145

Ante, pp. 187, 188.

We cannot wholly avoid, though unwilling to follow at great length, the old discussion which began when Grouchy and Gérard first differed at Sart-les-

Walhain, as to the expediency of the cross-march
which the latter proposed. It is impossible to lay
down certainly what would have been the precise
effect on the close of the day's operations had the
Marshal taken his junior's advice, and moved by
Mousty on Plancenoit. Those whose opinions are on
all accounts entitled to respect differ absolutely here.

Jom.
p. 224.

Jomini believes such a march might have had at least
a moral weight, though he well remarks that its supposed effect upon the Prussian proceedings can be but

Cha.p.321.

conjecture at the best. Charras maintains broadly
that neither an earlier march, nor better manœuvring
on Grouchy's part, could have averted the catastrophe

Claus.
p. 172.

of Waterloo. Clausewitz, viewing Grouchy in the
simple light of the agent of Napoleon's orders to
pursue the Prussians, declares that for him to have
turned away from Blücher's track, and marched to the
point where another part of the French were known
to be engaged with another enemy, would have been
contradictory alike to sound theory and practice. As
the discussion, however, certainly arose when the
firing was heard, it is well to examine briefly what
the possibilities were on which so much criticism of
Grouchy's operations has been based. As Quinet

Quin.
p. 298.

points out, Napoleon at St. Helena assumed that the
Marshal was two hours' march from Waterloo, General
Valazé (Grouchy's engineer) three hours, Gérard four
and a half, and Jomini five ; whilst Charras makes
the distance eight or nine hours' march. To settle
this vexed question, Quinet procured an itinerary of

the actual road proposed for Grouchy's troops, and found that *a single passenger on foot*, walking quickly, from Sart-les-Walhain by Mousty to Plancenoit, *takes five hours and a half.* From this he very properly concludes, that the estimate of Charras is by no means an excessive one for the movement of a corps d'armée ; and this practical examination at once explodes the visions conjured up to eager French minds then and now by ' the country people ' whom Thiers quotes as promising Grouchy to conduct him to the field in a four hours' march. A little farther on than this passage, the same historian himself fixes the limit of time within which Grouchy must have arrived to be of service, as from six to seven hours, and thus unconsciously settles the question against himself, whether the supposed march is calculated from the itinerary of the road, or by the not less sure method of comparing it to that actually made by Bülow along a similar line. This latter general started, as before shown, at 7 a.m., lost two hours owing to the fire in Wavre, and collected his whole corps before Plancenoit at half-past five, having actually occupied in the operation eight hours and a half. Grouchy, at Sart-les-Walhain, had just three miles further to move as the crow flies, and it was near noon when the march was proposed. Tried by the test of the Prussian marching, the proposed advantage of his flank movement fails as certainly as if examined by the simpler proof of Quinet.

Thiers and his school will not abandon for one

Thi. xx. 260.

Ibid. 263.

Ante, pp. 167, 173.

Belg. Gov. Survey.

rebuff their attempt to throw the weight of the French strategical failure of the day from the Emperor on his lieutenant. Grouchy need not, according to their view, have gone to Plancenoit at all. An intermediate march across the Dyle at Limal would have surprised the Prussians on the way, by taking them perpendicularly, in flank. This case, however, admits of simple treatment, and indeed has been fully considered by theorists favourable to Napoleon. Jomini stands at the head of these, and his decision is as follows :—

Thi. xx. 265.

'Nevertheless, we must be allowed to believe that, in any event, the Prussian Marshal, after having observed Grouchy's force, would have judged the divisions of Pirch and Thielemann sufficient to hold it back, whilst with those of Bülow and Zieten he aided Wellington to decide the victory.' To this opinion we need only add the remark that Thielemann alone did actually for six hours afford Grouchy that resistance, to offer which Jomini declares would at the most have occupied his corps and that of Pirch.

Jom. p. 223.

Müffling, writing upon this subject but a few months after the battle, when Grouchy's wing was overrated, being reckoned at 45,000 men, speaks with much plainness on this subject. The direct march of the Marshal by Limal on St. Lambert, he declares would have put the Prussian army in a very hazardous position had Wellington already been beaten. From this he draws the conclusion, that 'an experienced general' (if Grouchy had attempted

Müff. Hist. p. 67.

this) ' would infer that the safest operation was to collect the three corps on the march towards Waterloo, and attack Napoleon at once.' If this be the correct view, it proves that Blücher acted in the wisest possible way, even in case of the worst combination of circumstances conceivable against his side. What is practically more important is to note that the orders Blücher gave, when his rear was Ante, p. 176. actually attacked, were precisely in the spirit here indicated by the theorist.

Charras, who examines very thoroughly the whole Cha. p. 320, 321. controversy—the most important of those which concern us—declares that Grouchy's great inferiority to the Prussians debarred his being an element of any weight in the calculations of the day ; that if he had started ever so early, and manœuvred ever so dexterously, the disaster of Waterloo would not have been less certain or less complete. If we reject this view on account of the animus of the gifted author, we must with it set aside the vision conceived by the Napoleonist writers of Grouchy swooping down on the flank of the surprised Prussians ; since these Prussians outnumbered him threefold, were observing him from high ground, and had occupied from the morning before the whole intervening district with their patrols. Reverting, then, to the moderate critics of whom Jomini is the type, we may sum up the discussion by declaring that in no case could Grouchy, according to a fair theoretical view, have in any way stopped more than two of the

o

four Prussian corps, and that, judging from the actual facts as they occurred, he would hardly have stopped more than one.

All this is on the supposition that Grouchy had a right to judge for himself. This, however, is more than doubtful under the circumstances. Not two hours before the discussion at Walhain, Napoleon had Ante, p. 165. dispatched plain instructions bearing the order, ' You are to direct your movements on Wavre, in order to come near to us.' The same letter stated that the Emperor was about to attack the English army at Waterloo. Suppose that Grouchy had been able, by a magic glance, to read the words of this letter in the hands of the yet far-off messenger, why should he, on hearing that the Emperor's battle had begun, turn aside from the road to Wavre, to draw near to Napoleon by some other ? In fact, if Grouchy was wrong, Napoleon must have been far more wrong than he. Claus. p. 157. Kenn. p. 160. This truth, first seized by Clausewitz, has been put into the clearest light by Kennedy, whose words on this subject need no addition :

' Napoleon had positive and certain knowledge of the existence of a general action, and was free to give to Grouchy what orders he chose ; Grouchy, on the contrary, could only guess as to the existence of a general action, and in acting upon a probable supposition would have done so contrary to his instructions. Now, Napoleon not only failed to send any order to Grouchy to march upon Waterloo, when he knew positively that he was about to engage in a general action

with the Anglo-Allied army; but even when the
action was actually commencing, he caused Soult to
write to him approving of his marching upon Wavre.
If, then, Grouchy violated a principle in not marching
to the field of battle, Napoleon violated the same
principle, and in an aggravated degree, by not ordering his march upon Waterloo early on the morning of
the 18th; and in going the length of approving of his
march upon Wavre when the battle of Waterloo was
actually commencing.' *The fact is* (as this writer
goes on to say) *that Napoleon did not the least foresee
the flank march of the Prussians.* The written corre- Ante,
spondence clearly proves that Grouchy thought to p. 144.
separate them from Wellington by marching on
Wavre; and that Napoleon's letters—not this one of
10 a.m. only but that of 1 p.m.—distinctly approve Ante, p.
the Marshal's intention. The notion that Grouchy is 165, 174.
responsible for the Waterloo defeat must be dismissed,
by those who choose to weigh the evidence, from the
domain of authentic history to the limbo of national
figments.

It need hardly be said that these orders of the
18th to Grouchy are not quoted textually by Thiers.
They are spoken of by him as ambiguous and vague, Thi. xx.
as taking a long time in Soult's hands to dispatch, as 194.
not being worth the hour thus lost. Napoleon is supposed throughout these operations, in the theory of
his defenders, to have lost the power of supervising and
controlling the actions of the subordinates nearest to
him. But in truth the language of the order reveals

the mind of him who ordered, as plainly as did those of the day before ; and if any doubt were left of the utter state of ignorance which the Emperor was in as to the strategy of his enemies, it should be dispelled

Thi. xx. 200, and ante. p. 173.

when we find him, on the confession of his best advocates, utterly unsuspicious of what the apparition at St. Lambert meant, and contenting himself, until the capture of Bülow's messenger, with a detachment of light cavalry to observe it.

From the moment that the truth became known to him, the Prussian march influenced the tactics at Waterloo. Although writing to Grouchy of Bülow's corps only, as though he could not realise the full

Ante, pp. 173, 176.

weight of the coming blow, ten thousand men were at once withdrawn from his reserves, the infantry being the two intact divisions of Lobau ; and these were not long afterwards supported by the choicest troops of the Guard. From the time of the capture of the letter, it must be held in fairness that the fighting forces of the French, as against Wellington, were reduced by the whole of those thus destined to another

Ante, p. 145 and p. 180.

purpose, and were, therefore, brought down practically to 56,000 men.

Admitting this, there was still an undoubted superiority on the assailant's side—a superiority not numerical indeed, yet not the less real ; and until the arrival of Zieten's advance-guard, the English General

Gourg. p. 87. Cha.p.260. Brial. ii. 427.

had no aid against this. We must inquire therefore, briefly, into the causes which enabled him to hold his ground until the relief was given him, which, in

the opinion of Continental writers, first turned suc- Muff. His p. 34.
cessful resistance into victory, as the pressure of Claus. p. 168.
Bülow's attack made the latter the completest ever Austr. Report, Doc. 102.
imagined.

To judge of these causes, let us look to the excuses Spanish ditto, Doc. 106.
given by Napoleon for his defeat in his earliest and
most authentic narrative. These are as clearly and
forcibly laid down by the ex-Emperor as though he Gourg. p. 93.
were writing simple truths for the philosophic student
of history, instead of weaving fictions suited to
national vanity. The first and chiefest concerns the
conduct of Grouchy, which we have already considered,
and turns, in fact, wholly on the strategy. There are
two others given which belong to the actual tactics
of the long day's struggle against Wellington, and,
briefly, they are these. The first, the unseasonable
attack made by Ney with the cavalry two hours too
soon, in spite of the repeated orders of the Emperor ;
the second, the want of a general at the head of the
whole Guard.

This story as to Ney's fault has been seriously
taken up by Thiers, or it would be hardly worthy our Thi. ix. 225, &c.
deliberate notice. It is a melancholy instance of the
perversion of history to suit national fancy, that would
represent such a chief as Napoleon, sitting in the midst
of a great action, fought on a narrow space, sur-
rounded by an ample staff, and served by officers of
unequalled experience, and yet unable to restrain his
lieutenants from uselessly sacrificing his troops at
the wrong seasons. We may be sure that neither

Napoleon nor his advocates would have admitted such an excuse for any other general's defeat, except at the price of admitting that general to be hopelessly incompetent for the work he had undertaken. For the rest, Colonel Heymès has fully explained the particulars of the cavalry attack, which was in great part not ordered by Ney, but undertaken by the reserves of that arm, who vainly imagined the British centre in retreat. From his account we need only quote the simple words (which no evidence has ever touched), 'but this movement was executed under the eyes of the Emperor; he might have stopped it; he did not do so,' to show on whom the real responsibility lies.

Mém. ix. 268.

As to the absence of any successor to Mortier with the Guards, considering that Napoleon had this corps under his immediate eye the whole of the earlier part of the battle, ranged the last portion of it in array himself, and personally ordered its earlier detachments, this so-called cause of his defeat shows as the very poorest shadow of excuse a beaten general ever offered, and is indeed left untouched by critics, hostile and friendly, as though not worthy any serious consideration.

Mém. ix. 141.

We need not search the various histories far without lighting on something more tangible. Jomini and Charras, from their very different points of view, condemn alike the employment of the infantry of Reille and D'Erlon in unmanageable masses unaided by cavalry, as well as the third attack, by cavalry alone

Cha.p.291.
Jom.
p. 230.

without infantry. The latter of these critics reminds us further that the fourth and only partially successful advance, that made through La Haye Sainte, was unsupported. Kennedy, who treats this part of the battle with special care and vigour, has not only, as before shown, pointed this out, but condemned Napoleon for directing his final reserves, when he did move them, up to another part of the British line which was abundantly prepared to receive them. In fact, the famous charge of the Guard was altogether an insufficient effort for the end in view. The battalions actually engaged vary from four to nine in the various French accounts, and were utterly unsupported, the portion held in reserve being arrested by the disturbance caused on the French right by Zieten's advance, and the rest of the infantry and cavalry already, as all accounts admit, exhausted in the fruitless attacks which had preceded this. In plain truth, Napoleon's tactical performance on this great day was not only inferior to that of his antagonist, but beneath his own previous reputation. To sum it up in the words of a writer whose spirit often inclines strongly to the side of Napoleon, even where he writes the praises of his opponent : ' He made the first attack against La Haye Sainte with over-deep masses ; he engaged, or allowed to be engaged, his cavalry too soon ; finally, he showed some hesitation when, at six o'clock, he had the proof that a general effort on the centre might succeed. Nor was this effort made with enough troops, or sufficient unity. *In general, all the attacks*

Ante, p. 175.

Kenn. p. 127, 167.

Vaudoncourt (in Loben S. p. 299). Thi. xx. 242. Quin. p. 256-262. Cha.p.255.

Thi. xx. 244. Cha.p.259.

Brial. ii. 438.

made during this day had the defect of being badly supported.'

How greatly Wellington's conduct in this regard contrasts with that of his rival we have already shown, and need not enlarge on it further ; but another chief cause of his success which should never be forgotten was the staunch conduct of his heroic British infantry.

Ante, p. 175.

It seems hardly right to pass from this subject without some notice of the long-standing controversy relative to the shares borne in the repulse of the Imperial Guard by the respective regiments engaged. The discussion here has been made to turn, much more than is necessary for settling the real issue, upon the minor question, *whether there were two distinct columns, or only one divided into two portions.* For in the former case it is admitted that one must have been routed by the English Guards : in the latter, that more favourable to those who claim the whole glory of the affair for the 52nd, it is asserted that the real head of the column did not reach the crest ; that the Guard only came into collision with its skirmishers ; and that the 52nd alone decided this part of the battle, defeating singly a single attack.

See Leeke, ch. v. &c.

The weight of general testimony is strongly in favour of the former opinion. The best French authorities are decided on this point ; although Thiers, following the mythic narrative of his disaster bequeathed by Napoleon, makes the second column not far enough advanced to meet the hostile infantry.

Cha. p. 255. &c. Quin, p. 260–262. Thi. xx. 245–246. Gourg. p. 101–102.

The Dutch historian, writing from a comparison of the original French reports with those of his own country-men, many of whom were with the British right and centre, is equally certain in this matter. Against these must be placed the strong but isolated testi-mony of the officers of the 52nd, and especially that of (Colborne) Lord Seaton. Yet if their view of the French formation be accepted as correct, we find that even they admit that a formidable body of skir-mishers, thrown out by the attacking column, was checked by Maitland and his Guards. Mr. Leeke, the champion of the 52nd, further suggests that these skirmishers were probably joined by those of Donze-lot's division, co-operating with the column on its right; and he speaks of them as ' a numerous body,' and again as ' a large mass,' declaring that the Guards formed line against them and drove them some way down the slope. The distance between this mass and the actual head of the column he makes ' about 100 yards; ' but he adds, that, although the French column ' was being played upon by our artillery 300 yards above, there appeared to be no confusion among them. It was not until the 52nd skirmishers fired into them that they halted.' Admitting this description to be written in the utmost good faith, it amounts to no more than an expression of the strong belief of Mr. Leeke and his comrades, that the column, although such a near witness to the repulse of its own advance, and suffering from a close artillery fire, cared for neither of these, but was checked solely by

Loben S. p. 299.

Leeke, i. ch. v. U. S. Mag. 1868, vol. i. (Art. by Sir J. Alex-ander).

Leeke, i. 75.

Ibid. 42, 43.

Ibid.

Ibid. 45.

For example (as Lord Seaton), Leeke, i. 101.

Letter
quoted by
Leeke, i.
100.
Ibid. i. 84.

See origi-
nal in U.S.
Journal,
1833, vol.
ii. 302.

MS. Jour-
nal of
Lt.-Gen.
Sir H.
Clinton,
communi-
cated to
the
author.

See note
at foot.

their flank attack.   That ' the [English] Guards made some forward movement,' Lord Seaton himself supposes.   Colonel Gawler, whose evidence on other points Mr. Leeke uses, and who himself wrote his ' Crisis of Waterloo ' to claim the whole credit for the 52nd, admits that ' the headmost companies of the Imperial Guard crowned the very summit of the position, and their dead bodies the next day bore unanswerable evidence to the fact.'   These statements have all been made public long since ; but there is one not so known, yet decisive of the real question, by Sir H. Clinton, general of the division to which the 52nd belonged, whose journal for the 18th June, dated the same day, distinctly records his own impression, that the Guards chiefly received and repulsed the attack, but that the brigade to which the 52nd belonged followed up the repulse.*   To suppose this

---

* The passage runs as follows, and is doubly important as showing the impression at the moment of the value of the Prussian assistance on the minds of the higher officers of the British staff: ' About 7 p.m. the enemy appeared to be decidedly beaten, and our artillery was nearly exhausted ; but finding the Prussians, whose attack on his right commenced about 5½ o'clock, to be gaining ground, and unable to make a good retreat in the presence of two armies which had been successful, Buonaparte determined to make one great effort to compel the Duke of Wellington to retire.   For this object he brought forward his Imperial Guards and reinforced all his batteries, which he advanced and began his attack with.   *The weight of this was directed against the brigade of Guards.   It was steadily received and repulsed,* and the enemy was followed up by the brigade of General Adams [of which the 52nd formed part] supported by the Osnabruck battalion, the Legion, 23rd Regiment &c.   We had no sooner gained the Genappe road than the enemy abandoned everything and took to his heels ; but as there was still a large body of cavalry I kept the Legion and 23rd Regiment in reserve, and con-

wholly inaccurate, is to suppose that Sir H. Clinton, writing long before Wellington's dispatch was published, robbed his own division of certain credit due them to bestow it on the Guards, whose claim, Leeke, i. 80. according to their opponents, originated in the omission and mistakes of that dispatch.

This evidence seems conclusive against the claims of the 52nd to have singly defeated the French Guard, however formed. Enough remains for that famous regiment, already high in the roll of history, whose splendid flank attack and steady pursuit, with the final overthrow of the intact battalions which it met at the foot of the hill, prove that neither Colborne nor his men were overpraised in the glowing pages of the ' Peninsular War.' The Dutch have assigned Loben S. p. 299. much of the credit here to Chassé's division, which opportunely reinforced the line about the time of the assault ; but the proof is undeniable, from the testi- Quin. p. 262. See various evidences cited by Gawler and Leeke on this point. mony of numerous eye-witnesses, that Colborne, keeping steadily in advance of the rest of the Anglo-Allied infantry, defeated the only battalions left unbroken of the Guard, whether forming their reserve, or part of the second column.

That Wellington failed either to acknowledge this See his conversa- tion with Gurwood, Leeke, i. 97. service in his dispatch, or to repair the omission in later days, shows strongly how wanting he was in that sympathy with the human craving for applause, without which no general's character could be

tinued to advance. In the road I met with some Prussians, who had the same success on their side.'—*Journal of Sir H. Clinton (communicated by his nephew through General Lindsay)*.

complete. The brave infantry, whose constancy in battle helped to place him high on the roll of world-famous commanders, met with scanty praise from his lips, though their conduct won them tributes of admiration alike from foe and from ally. The testimony of Marshal Bugeaud to the unparalleled worth of these troops is well known, and General Trochu in his work on the French Army has reminded us specially of it : but that of Müffling is here even more important, since it cannot be a matter of interest to any Prussian writer to exalt beyond due measure the share in the glory of the day due to British firmness. We quote it therefore in full :

See 'L'Armée Française en 1867,' 19th ed. p. 35.

'For a battle, there is not perhaps in Europe an army equal to the British ; that is to say, none whose tuition, discipline, and whole military tendency is so purely and exclusively calculated for giving battle. The British soldier is vigorous, well fed, by nature brave and intrepid, trained to the most rigorous discipline, and admirably well armed. The infantry resist the attacks of the cavalry with great confidence, and when taken in the flank or rear, British troops are less disconcerted than any other European army.

Müff. Hist. p. 81.

'These circumstances in their favour will explain how this army, since the Duke of Wellington conducted it, has never yet been defeated in the open field.'

No account of the great day of Waterloo could be

complete which did not speak, and speak plainly, of
the strategical error with which Wellington is charged
in leaving 18,000 of his troops detached to his right
at Hal and Tubize,* thereby wilfully reducing his
army to a numerical inferiority to that of Napoleon.
Any military act of the Duke's at this great era finds
abundance of advocates. He also has taken some
pains to defend himself in that 'Memorandum' in
reply to Clausewitz, to which we have so often referred, but which is not sufficiently accurate in its
details, as has been already pointed out, to have the
due weight which any contribution of Wellington's to ^{Ante, p.}
the history of the campaign would have had, had he ^{79, 123, 153.}
written whilst events were fresh in his memory. It
seems that in his old age he had unhesitatingly
accepted the story told in Napoleon's 'Mémoires,' ^{Mém. ix.}
that a French detachment of cavalry really sought to ^{101.}
turn his right on the 17th, and induced him to keep
this body of troops on that side all the next day. If
so, it would appear therefore that he had fallen at last
into a trap laid by Napoleon, since this story is so
utterly unsubstantiated by evidence as to be neglected
by the ordinary school of French writers, and denied
by the more veracious. In fact such a cavalry
detachment not being made, could not be heard of, and
could certainly be no excuse for Wellington. It was
simply one of the many inventions of the later St.

* At Hal alone, according to most writers; but Colville's two
brigades remained halted at Tubize on the way to Hal. *Vide*
Sib. i. 356.

Helena version, put forth after Wellington's singuar occupation of Hal became known to Napoleon in his exile, in order to gain the latter credit for deceiving his antagonist. The Duke's conduct must be judged on its own merits, and it is sufficient here to say that all Continental critics (with one exception to be noted presently) agree in condemning it absolutely : that the best of the recent English professional writers to the full agree with them : and that Müffling, in attempting faintly to excuse it, has only done so by elaborately proving that the troops thus detached could have equally well observed the Hal road had they been stationed behind the Senne, two hours nearer to Waterloo from Hal, and that, at any rate, they should have been called in so as to arrive on the 18th by noon. This being the best defence in support of the Duke's peculiar view, which led him to guard himself in the direction of his communications at a present risk of sacrificing the real object of the day, we might conclude unhesitatingly by subscribing to the broad assertion of Kennedy, ' that Wellington ought certainly to have had Colville, with the force under his command, on the field of battle,' but for the possibility already dwelt on of the separation of his right wing by his centre being forced, and his own retreat being made to his left. In this supposed case, when the troops at Hal might have been useful to cover the wing thus cut off, lies the best excuse suggested for the apparent sacrifice.

It has been urged, in opposition to this view, that

Kenn. p. 174.

Hamley (Well. Career), p. 82.

Müff. Hist. p. 78.

See ante, p. 186.

Wellington knew himself able to maintain his ground without the troops detached. But Wellington could not possibly have known that morning that Napoleon would grant the Prussians five hours' fair start, nor that he would withdraw 16,000 of the French from his attacking force to meet them, instead of pressing on his reserves at an earlier part of the day. The presence of Colville's brigades might have kept the British line from that 'critical' hour which all Continental eye-witnesses declared to have occurred before Zieten came up, and which General Ziegler expressly reports that the Duke himself admitted six years later. On the other hand, it may well be remarked, that this blot is the single one of several once charged against Wellington for that day's conduct, which time has not long since cleared away ; for the mistake, which he admitted himself to have made, in neglecting to strengthen La Haye Sainte, he repaired on the spot by personal exertion when he found it a cause of danger. The pierced walls of Hougoumont, though hastily prepared, did admirable service through the day, as has always been admitted ; whilst certain orders issued* for the more general fortifying of the position,

Side notes: See the various passages referred to, ante, p. 196. Büd. p. 10.

For such see particularly replies in Müff. Hist.

Kenn. p. 175.

Ante, p. 175.

See Mem. of Sir H. Clinton in note below.

---

* As this fact has hitherto been wholly ignored it is as well to quote the original authority in full. 'About 11 A.M. the Light Brigade and German Legion were ordered to furnish working parties to throw up breastworks to cover our guns ; but when they arrived the officer with the intrenching tools was not present, and before these works were begun the enemy had commenced his attack. So the guns had no cover.'—Extract from Memoranda left by Sir H. Clinton on the position, &c., of the 2nd Division at Waterloo, communicated by his family with the journal quoted at page 202.

For ex-
ample, Sir
F. Head in
his 'Royal
Engineer,'
p. 327–
329.
though unexecuted for lack of time and means, prove
that the English General was not so disposed as some
recent critics have alleged, to overlook the resources
which art might have lent to his purpose. In fine,
the noble concert of operations between the Allies,
with the tactical readiness of Wellington, fully atoned
for his one error of strategy. The great victory was
no chance issue, as French vanity would make it ; nor
the mere spoil, as some of our countrymen have
thought, of dogged, unaided courage. To those who
look fairly at its history, it stands proved the fairly
won prize of a combination of valour, skill, and mutual
support, such as the world had never witnessed before
in allied armies led by independent generals.

Summary.

The events of June 18th are not so intricate in
reality as overlaid and made obscure by controversy.
An impartial examination of the evidence on either
side brings out clearly the following facts, the proofs
of which have been already given.

Whilst Wellington calmly waited the attack of his
enemy, secure in the present goodness of his position
and of the succour promised him by Blücher, Napoleon, all ignorant of the Allied design, believed he had
but to deal with the 70,000 troops before him, and
spent the first half of the day in delay and parade,
with the double purpose of allowing the ground to dry
up partially, and of imposing on the weak and doubtful contingents by a show of strength. Meanwhile,

the Prussians, though starting less early than was intended, were, for the most part, well upon their way to the field, where Bülow might have arrayed all his divisions early in the afternoon, but for the accident of their delay in the streets of Wavre, and the mistake of posting them, though they were to lead the march, on the wrong side of that town the night before. Grouchy, starting at the same hour as the Prussians, had moved from Gembloux on Sart-les-Walhain, uncertain at first how far northward he should push in his search for them; but, soon gathering information that they had actually gone to Wavre in great force, he resolved to continue his march thither. He had received no instructions from his master since the written order to proceed to Gembloux : and the single letter, dispatched to him that morning, after stating that the Emperor was about to engage the English, ordered him to move on Wavre, and to follow up by light troops the enemy's columns which had gone to his right ; showing that Napoleon, like his lieutenant, attached little importance to the district between them to the latter's left, where the Prussian outposts really lay. Long before this letter was received the sound of the battle was heard, and the Marshal was pressed to march towards the firing : his decision not to do this, but to go on to Wavre where the Prussians were last heard of, was the natural consequence of the original orders which he had received, directing him to pursue them, and exactly anticipated those which were on their way. Had he chosen otherwise he

P

might possibly have become engaged with, and detained, two corps of the Prussians, instead of the one which he fought afterwards at Wavre ; but to suppose him justified in doing this is simply to suppose that he knew better than Napoleon himself, what Napoleon wished at the time that the battle began.

Meanwhile the Emperor, having thus directed Grouchy on a line upon which that day he could be of no immediate service in the action, commenced it by his first attack, that made upon the British right and Hougoumont. This was only preparatory to the second, the essay of D'Erlon's strong and intact corps against the British left. Before this last began, the leading division of Bülow showed itself at St. Lambert : but though it was seen by Napoleon, his 1 p.m. letter to Grouchy, written at this juncture with the vagueness of indecision, permitted the march to Wavre to go on, yet directed the Marshal (an order contradictory to this approval) to manœuvre towards the Emperor's right, so as to be ready to crush any hostile troops which might seek to disturb it. A sudden postscript, added on the capture of the Prussian messenger, revealed the fatal truth now first understood, and called on Grouchy for instant help. Yet even then Napoleon ignored to his lieutenant, and probably to himself, the advance of any other enemies than the single corps of Bülow. And this letter, though a horseman might have ridden through by-roads to Grouchy in two hours, was not delivered until 6 or 7 p.m., when the Marshal was irretrievably committed to the battle at Wavre, and that at Waterloo practically decided. To meet the new danger Napoleon detached 10,000 of his reserve, increased afterwards to 16,000, to cover his right rear. No attempt was made to arrest the enemy in their passage over the deep valley of the Lasne : yet so difficult was this by nature, and so many the obstacles to Blücher's movement, that it took three hours from the first appearance of Bülow on St. Lambert before half his corps were brought into action. For three hours more an action of great severity raged between him and the troops of Lobau, decided only finally by the coming up of Pirch to the support of the assailants.

The second attack of the French having been decisively repulsed by Picton's infantry, their cavalry unsupported engaged the British centre. The murderous loss to that splendid arm which resulted from their useless assaults of our squares, was not actually the consequence of Napoleon's orders, nor of Ney's : but both permitted the vain charges to be repeated until the horsemen were all but totally destroyed. The fourth grand attack, made by infantry under Ney's direction, lodged the French in La Haye Sainte, and penetrated for a moment the British line beyond. But Napoleon, either restrained by Blücher's pressure on Plancenoit, or not discerning his advantage in time, held his last reserve back ; and Wellington skilfully repaired the gap.

Zieten soon afterwards appeared on the extreme

English left, releasing two brigades of cavalry not yet engaged, which did good service soon after in the final rout. After some short delay caused by a mistake, he formed a decisive attack upon the right wing of the French and routed it, just as the small body of reserve which Napoleon had kept in hand to the last made the final attempt upon the English right centre, which has been well called ' the last madness of despair.' There is no reason to believe that this attack of the Guard could have shaken the line of Wellington, which was thoroughly made up at that point by troops brought in from the extreme wings. If the British army was actually in a critical state that day (as the testimony of all witnesses but those of its own nation goes to prove), it was at an earlier period, just after the enemy had carried La Haye Sainte. The effect produced on the French by the repulse of the Guard and the sudden onslaught of Zieten, was completed by the general advance, for which Wellington, with the instinct of genius, suddenly forsook his attitude of defence ; and defeat was turned into a tide of panic and an unexampled rout when Blücher's columns soon after poured through Plancenoit across the sole line of escape open to the fugitives.

See the authorities referred to, ante, p. 196.

If Wellington in this battle had shown some over-confidence in the needless detachment which weakened his line, the energy of his Ally, the firmness of his choicer troops, his own masterly adroitness in tactics, had redeemed the error if they did not wholly justify

it. Nor let it be forgotten by English writers, that
to the early display of Prussian force it was due that
their countryman's battle was waged against an army
less by 16,000 than Napoleon had drawn up ; nor
that the ardour of our Ally to redeem the delays of
the road and share in the combat, cost Blücher's
forces just 7,000 men in an action which lasted barely 6,999 by Pr. Off. p. 85.
four hours. Of Napoleon on the 18th June it stands
clearly proved, that his management of the attacks
was so imperfect that his advocates would fain charge
the details to his lieutenants ; that he neglected the
only hope of arresting Blücher at the passage of the
Lasne ; and that he prolonged the battle uselessly
until safe retreat was impossible. To sum up
shortly : had it been any other general that acted
thus on that eventful day, it would long ago have
been plainly said, that his tactics in the battle were
as defective as the strategy which placed him in it at
such fearful odds.

LECTURE VII.

THE RETREAT OF GROUCHY TO FRANCE.—COMMENTS. —CONCLUDING REFLECTIONS.—SUMMARY OF THE CAMPAIGN.

To follow the broken fortunes of Napoleon and his soldiery beyond the night of their great disaster would be of small profit for our purpose. The best comment on the completeness of the ruin which befell them is contained in the simple mention of the occurrences which pressed closely on his heels. Deserting the wreck of his army, the Emperor fled to Paris, hoping apparently, when once more at the seat of government, to rally a force sufficient to defend it, at least for a time. If these illusions were really entertained by him (whose restless brain had held many schemes as wild), they were not shared by his few supporters. Neither he nor his faithful troops were destined again to draw sword in the lost cause of the Empire. Arriving, on the third morning after the battle, at the agitated capital, scarcely recovered from the tremendous shock which the first news of Waterloo inflicted, Napoleon plunged for the last time into the maze of politics, to the domain of

Thi. xx. 338.

which the history of the following events belongs. It is sufficient for our purpose to add, that the tide set so strongly against him as to force him to abdicate on the following day, the 22nd. A week later, he was a fugitive from Paris, whither the vengeful Prussians were pressing in hopes of seizing his person, and where the Provisional Government of the hour refused all his offers of advice or service. Leaving him on his way to the hopeless exile which was a necessary condition for the peace of the world, we turn back to review the last of the military events connected with his irruption into Belgium. Thi. xx. 437, 439.

These do not relate to the troops overthrown at Waterloo. It would profit us little to know how many of the fugitives gathered at Philippeville, how many at Laon, or who took the chief share in rallying them. A mass of soldiers formed of the fragments of regiments and corps deprived of their officers, their arms thrown away, and suffering themselves from the depressing influence of utter defeat, could count for little as obstacles to the victorious torrent pouring into France across her northern frontier. It would be to add to the curiosities of military litera-ture, and not its useful lessons, were we to trace in detail the exact numbers that were collected, and the different leaders they obeyed. Let us turn rather to follow that distinct and unbroken force under Grouchy which had escaped partaking in the national disaster.

We left this Marshal after a sharp encounter, begun some hours later than the battle of Waterloo, Ante, p. 181.

and prolonged until dark, with the passage of the Dyle at Limal in his hands, though it was won too late to pass over more than the left wing of his army. He had no news of the Emperor since the missive came which was closed on the capture of Bülow's messenger. He was left, therefore, for the night to indulge in the extreme of hope or fear, as fancy might lead him.

Pr. Off.
p. 94.
Claus.
p. 138 (at
3 a.m. by
Grouchy's
Report,
Doc. 153.)

At break of day, Thielemann, believing it still possible to recover the lost passage, attacked the French before Limal with all the troops in hand. But Grouchy had used the hours of the night to defile his divisions across the stream, and was in far superior force upon the left bank. The Prussians were easily repulsed, and the French Marshal, still ignorant of his master's fall, deployed on the ground just won with methodical care, and took the offensive with resistless strength. In vain the Prussian general, driven from his first position, took up a second near to Wavre. This, too, had just been

Pr. Off.
p. 95.

carried, when, between 8 and 9 a.m., authentic intelligence reached him from Pirch of the great result of the day before. In hopes of checking the still sharp

Claus.
p. 139.

pressure of Grouchy, he caused his troops to cheer loudly, and to advance in their turn as though already in receipt of succour. The French, on their side, either did not understand the signal, or chose to discredit it, and the battle went on unslackened. Wavre was now abandoned to them, and a third position occupied by Thielemann. But a fresh force of

French (part of Vandamme's troops) debouching through the town, turned this also by its left, and made their enemy fall back a third time, and begin Pr. Off. p. 97. a regular retreat to the north-east by the Louvain road, which he justly hoped soon to change for a pursuit when Grouchy should learn the truth. This reached the Marshal about 11 a.m., when, according Ibid. and Doc. 154. to his own narrative, he was preparing (for he considered the enemy now retiring to be disposed of for the present) to turn westward to his left and march direct upon Brussels. The messenger dispatched by Napoleon the night before from near Charleroi to carry the tidings of his defeat, told the Marshal that such force as was left to the Emperor was retreating to the Sambre. Hardly had Grouchy checked his ad- Ibid. vance when he learnt that the Prussians were already upon that river, and occupying the whole country to his left flank and rear. Their advance in fact, as we Ante, p. 181. have seen, thanks to Gneisenau's unceasing energy, had pushed within a few miles of Charleroi before daylight; nor, whilst occupied with the direct pursuit of the beaten Emperor, had the Prussian Staff wholly forgotten that his Marshal yet remained to be dealt with. At the close of the battle, Pirch, whose corps had contributed so powerfully to the final success which carried Blücher on to the French line of retreat, was halted. His cavalry, indeed, was in great part employed with all other available horse to press the pursuit through Genappe towards Charleroi; Pr. Off. p. 84, 85. but, with the bulk of his troops, the general was directed to face about, and march across country on Sombreffe, in order to cut Grouchy off from the Sambre. This order was so far obeyed that the troops set off that night, crossing the Dyle as soon as it was fairly daylight, at the bridge of Bousval, and See Map. at 11 a.m. on the 19th had reached Mellery, a village nine miles in a direct line from Plancenoit, and barely Pr. Off. p. 85 and 99. Muff. Hist. p. 43. five over an open district from Sombreffe. As the men had been marching or fighting all the day before, it was absolutely necessary to halt here for rest and breakfast. Pirch had with him only 16,000 men ; a brigade of infantry, and all his cavalry except nine squadrons, having been carried off towards Genappe. Whilst he rested, his patrols were pushed out towards Wavre, but could only learn that the enemy were there in great force and still occupied Mont St. Guibert. Unable, or unwilling, in the absence of horse, to act in any enterprising manner, he resolved to wait for news of Thielemann, to whom Ibid. he sent various messengers ; but these were unable to get round or through the French, and his halt therefore lasted all the rest of the day.

About the same hour that Pirch reached Mellery, Ante, p. 217. Grouchy, as already shown, learnt his master's defeat and his own danger. The battle of Wavre had left him but 30,000 fighting men. To his right front were about 13,000 under Thielemann, whose losses had been heavy. To his left, towards St. Lambert, another body of Prussians had just appeared, being, in fact, no other than that division of Thielemann's

corps which had gone on towards Waterloo the day Ante, p. 170.
before, and had now turned back to try and aid their Pr. Off.
chief. Unknown numbers of the Prussians (Pirch's, p. 98.
in fact) were reported as on his flank, beyond Mont St. Grouchy in Doc.
Guibert ; and escape by the route over which the army p. 154.
had entered Belgium was altogether out of the question. The situation might well appear desperate to
the hardiest commander, and might almost have
justified the wild proposal attributed to Vandamme, Cha. p. 364.
of marching direct on Brussels, with the view of crossing the whole rear of the Allies, and escaping between
the western flank of their armies and the sea.
Grouchy's resolve was not only wiser than this, but
was fully justified by the success which followed it.

Of this unhappy soldier, long after he was laid in
the grave, the ablest and bitterest of the historians
who follow Napoleon in blackening his lieutenants'
names, has written thus : ' Gifted with coup d'œil
and vigour in action, he had no discernment in the
general direction of operations, and was especially
deficient in the sagacity necessary for the officer of
an advance-guard charged with the look-out of an Thi. xx. 173.
army.' We need hardly say that we are quoting
from Thiers, who thus attempts to assassinate his
victim's fame in the general, before commencing those
attacks in detail on his conduct during the eventful
march from Ligny to Wavre, which we have shown
to be as untenable in fact as unjust in spirit. Leaving controversy as to the possibilities of the two
previous days aside, it remains to be seen how the

Marshal really acted when left alone to his own judgment in the midst of victorious armies, with the roads over which the French had advanced already lost, his enemies aware of his dangerous condition, and no means of extricating himself from it but such as lay in a cool head and vigorous execution ; in short, in that very ' discernment in the general direction of operations ' in which the historian declares him especially deficient.

Retreat in the Charleroi direction being closed, that through the mass of the Ardennes seemed to present itself as the best means of escaping the Allied pursuit : but the French had no supplies which could maintain them in a country where subsistence was not to be picked up by the way. There remained but one hope. The fortress of Namur had been abandoned by the Prussians in their haste to concentrate on Ligny, and they had by their subsequent march northward left it uncovered. Could Grouchy once regain Sombreffe before the Prussians seized that point, he would have a clear passage along the great chaussée which led from Nivelles into the place, with an equally good one beyond it up the Meuse by which to escape ; and his rear, covered by the works, might file safely into France. Seizing rapidly at this hope, he dispatched his chief cavalry officer, General Exelmans, with seven regiments of dragoons, to ride at speed on Namur and seize the works. With Gérard's corps the Marshal followed, and by a forced march reached Sombreffe the same

Doc. 154.
Cha. p.
363.

evening, leaving Vandamme at Wavre to cover the rear. Thielemann had committed himself so far on the road to Louvain after his fight of the morning, that he decided not to move again this day, being Claus. (who was present) p. 140. ready to believe (according to the best testimony) that he could not miss overtaking the enemy's rear-guard on the morrow, and his soldiers being much exhausted by the long-continued and unequal engagement, in which his corps had lost 2,500 of its number. But Vandamme did not wait till morning should bring the attack. At 5 p.m. he commenced Pr. Off. p. 99. Cha. p. 365. his retreat unmolested, and at midnight took up his bivouac at Gembloux for a few hours' rest. His march was observed by the nearest division of the Prussians, that which had returned from St. Lambert Ante, p. 218. to rejoin Thielemann, and by them reported to the latter general, who gave orders to pursue at daylight.

On the 20th the French continued their retreat in Cha. pp. 366, 368, who writes from the reports in French archives. two columns. Vandamme, quitting Gembloux at 7 a.m. after a somewhat unnecessary delay, marched across country on Namur by a direct by-road. Grouchy, waiting probably till he knew his lieutenant to be on his way, moved from Sombreffe along the high road about the same hour. Both were attacked before they reached the fortress, the Marshal himself being overtaken a short distance from the fortress by the advance-guard of Pirch, which had left Mellery soon after 5 a.m., on learning that the enemy were Pr. Off. p. 100. moving on Namur. The same caution which had kept that general motionless all the day before, when within two hours' march of the road traversed by the retreating French, seems to have hampered him still. His troops did not succeed in engaging the enemy's rear-guard until 4 p.m., about which hour Thielemann's cavalry, having passed through Gembloux, overtook the tail of Vandamme's column, but, having no infantry with them, were enable to make any serious impression upon it. At 6 p.m. the whole of the French had passed within the works of Namur, with little loss but that of two or three light guns.

Pr. Off. p. 100. Cha. p. 368. Claus. p. 141. Indignant possibly at the result of his own slowness, Pirch directed an immediate assault upon the walls, in hopes of carrying the place before the enemy abandoned it : but Vandamme, entrusted by Grouchy Ibid. with the duty of covering with his own corps and Müff. Hist. p. 44. Teste's division the retreat of the army, defended the walls too vigorously for such a rash attack to succeed ; and after losing over 1,600 men, the Prussians desisted from an attempt which it is hard (according to their great national writer) to justify under Claus. p. 143. the circumstances. After this they pressed no more on Grouchy, who made his way unmolested up the See Map. Meuse to Dinant, and thence by Givet into the heart of France, having accomplished, with a very trifling loss, one of the most surprising escapes from a very critical position which modern history records. It was not until the 21st that his troops once more drew regular rations : nor did he receive any instructions Cha. p. 369. for his guidance till the 23rd, when orders from Soult directed him to continue his march on Soissons.

Comments.

The same hard master who was the first to assert
Grouchy's incompetence for command, has unconsciously left on record his own vivid impression at the
time of the imminence of the danger to which the
Marshal was abandoned. ' I have heard nothing at
all of Grouchy,' wrote Napoleon from Philippeville
in an often-quoted letter addressed to Joseph on the
day after his defeat. ' If he is not taken (as I fear
he is), I can get together in three days 50,000 men.'
Although the event was so different from the Emperor's anticipation, it will not surprise the student of
the Mémoires to find that, in the lengthy ' Observations ' they contain upon the events of the campaign,
not a word is given in praise of the condemned lieutenant's prompt and successful march. It is more
important for us here to note for warning how little
the class of French historians who follow the Exile of
St. Helena in his general views have improved upon
his candour. Thiers, who can find space to devote
sixteen pages to his arguments that Grouchy should
have marched direct on Waterloo, has given to the
whole particulars of the Marshal's escape just *thirty-
one lines*, and these so divided, without any appearance of art, into separate parts of his text, as to make
it difficult to trace this important operation (in which
at least 60,000 men were actually concerned) in the
history which glows with profuse and vivid details
of all other successful French marches ! Nor is this

See Orig.
in Cha. p.
335,
or Claus.
p. 143.

Thi. xx.
357, 368,
and 290,
294.

Ibid. 272
and 400.

dishonesty wholly of a negative character. His brief
narrative, so far from giving any credit to the Marshal,
is prefaced with the treacherous words, ' Grouchy,
who had been looked upon as lost, escaped from the
enemy by the most happy and unforeseen of chances.'
Truly, to write thus in cold blood of one long dead, is
to carry the animosity of personal controversy into
the very grave itself! It would seem, indeed, as
though he could not forgive Marshal Grouchy for
contradicting by his action during this episode of
the campaign the reproaches heaped upon him for
not divining better than his master the movements of
the Allies before the battle.

Charras, who is never content with vague criticism,
has declared that the second day's march of the
French on their retreat was less rapid than their
danger should have made it. The blame, however,
of the delay about Gembloux that morning is fixed
by him upon Vandamme, who kept his superior waiting for him—a fact that exonerates Grouchy from
this single imperfection alleged in his conduct of the
movement. This critic (here, as often, followed
almost literally by Hooper) does not omit to point
out, in the plainest terms, that the French escape was
rendered comparatively easy by negligence on the
part of Thielemann, and timidity on that of Pirch.
Had the former kept close to the French from the
moment they ceased to push him towards Louvain ;
had the latter not halted for more than an ordinary
rest at Mellery ; the one would have discovered the

Ante,
p. 221.
Cha. p.
366.

Ibid. p.
367.

Ante,
p. 221.

Ante,
p. 218.

retreat when it first began on the 19th, the other would have planted himself across their path, and placed them in the extremity of danger.

It is important here to see what is said of these shortcomings by the historians of the nation to which these generals belonged. Müffling then takes the fault off their shoulders to lay it rather on those of the headquarters staff. The general management of the pursuit he holds to have been wrong. Bülow's corps should have been employed for this purpose, and turned off from the Charleroi road at Quatre Bras as early as possible on the 19th. There is no doubt, in the view of this practical writer, that this corps might have reached Sombreffe by 7 a.m., and detaching thence 2,000 cavalry, 'taking as many infantry with them on their horses,' to seize Namur, might have gone on to Gembloux, and occupied that place with ease by noon. Had this been done, ' Grouchy would have been compelled to capitulate, or to die sword in hand.' On the other hand, as this had not been thought of at the close of the battle, ' when so total a defeat of the enemy could not have been anticipated,' it is not surprising that the faulty arrangement which detached Pirch with only part of a corps and uncertain instructions was not modified. The will of the soldier, that important element in war too often ignored by theorists and military historians, here came into force ; and to throw any additional pressure on a force already overworked was held a greater evil than to risk the escape of Grouchy.

Müff. Hist. p. 75.

Q

For the best troops are but men, and there is a point beyond which the instinct of a great commander will teach him not to force those under him by calling for impracticable exertions. As Müffling states it, with the practical view of one who had seen much service and reflected on what he had seen: ' Strong motives will be found by him who knows what it is to have troops under his command that had been incessantly marching and fighting, and who since the 18th had had hardly any rest or food, not hastily to alter dispositions which had been once adopted.' In such motives lies the best defence of Blücher and his staff for their omission.

Clausewitz is more severe than his countryman upon the conduct of Pirch, who, in his view, should have undoubtedly pushed on from Mellery to Namur on the 19th, and who, instead of wasting his men next day in the rash assault on the town, should have at once turned off to look for a separate passage over the Sambre, which would have brought him on to the flank of Grouchy's long column in its march to Dinant. ' But seldom,' he adds, ' in war is all done that might be done, and the task here assigned to General Pirch was anything but a common one, and would have called for a great degree of energy.' That no attempt was made by Blücher's staff to detach from Charleroi any of the force directly pursuing Napoleon is another fault noticed by this critic—yet hardly, in his view, strictly blameable, since, on the day after the battle, ' too little was known of Grouchy's situation to allow

Müff. Hist. p. 75.

Claus. pp. 142, 143.

the Allies to make the cutting him off a chief object in the forthcoming operations.' On Thielemann's share in the affair, Clausewitz, himself Quartermaster-General to that officer, makes no special comment. His narrative (as before noticed) states that Thielemann's troops were so thoroughly exhausted after their two days' engagement with Grouchy's large forces, that their chief decided absolutely on the 19th that he would not begin the pursuit that day. To say this, and to add that he expected to overtake them next day, is hardly to excuse it. The real fact is, that these Prussian chiefs of corps had been chosen (as was shown early in our narrative) chiefly for the reason of their certain subordination to Gneisenau, should Blücher be removed. They were unpractised in the separate and responsible commands which fell on them at this epoch, and which might possibly have been at any time beyond their powers. The Prussian Staff, in fact, had been formed not only to meet the wants of the State, but the demands of a mistaken professional feeling; and Grouchy reaped the full benefit of the error. Making every allowance for this advantage, and for the Prussian ignorance of his exact force * and position, is it not clear that his escape, begun without hesitation upon the exact point still left open, and brought, with disheartened troops, to such successful issue, shows this much-maligned general to have possessed a large share of that very

Ante, p. 216 Claus. p. 140.

Ante, p. 59.

---

* Several months later Grouchy was supposed by the Prussians to have had over 40,000 men. (See Müff. Hist. p. 27, *Note*.)

quality for high command of which Thiers declares him destitute ? Is it not also clear, to all who study the habits of French military historians, that, but for the special circumstances of the case, no praise would have been found too high for the energy and dexterity with which their countryman carried his force safely out of the very jaws of destruction ?

In truth, a candid survey of Grouchy's conduct, from the time of his first charge to his escape into France, shows two epochs in his character. His irresolution in the advance appears due solely to the vagueness of Napoleon's instructions, and the vast responsibility they placed on the Marshal, whilst his action was fettered by fear of transgressing them. Left to his own judgment he seems another man, and rises at once superior to the difficulties in which his master had plunged him. Even the one fault in his advance in which most writers agree—his movement on Gembloux without surveying the country to his left in the direction of Napoleon—was the literal fulfilment of the instructions which, even so late as 10 a.m. on the morning of the battle, made him follow up the enemy's columns ' which had gone to his right.' Napoleon, it may be said, was himself deceived by Grouchy's report of Prussians (Bülow's corps, no doubt) moving on that side : but Napoleon's own letter to Ney of the morning before, and his direction of Grouchy on Gembloux, show clearly that he had convinced himself that the bulk of the Prussians would do as he desired they should, and retire away from their Allies. In plain

Ante,
p. 165.

Ante, pp.
144, 145.

truth, never has a single reputation been so grossly sacrificed to salve national vanity as in this matter of Grouchy and Waterloo. So far from earning for him blame, the Marshal's conduct, weighing all the circumstances of the campaign, should have crowned his old age with honour. That the result has been so different, is due simply to the popular demand by the French for a scapegoat which should bear the shame cast upon them by their defeat, and to the readiness with which Napoleon supplied it in his lieutenant.

Concluding Reflections.

In closing our survey of this eventful contest there seem to be some points still remaining for final notice. Not that it is necessary to enter again into the particulars of the strategy. They have been fully considered as far as the scope of this work will admit, and it is needless to review them once more for any purpose of convincing the unwilling. He who maintains that Blücher had his corps disposed ready for the prompt concentration which events required ; or that Wellington made the best arrangements possible on the alarm for preventing the enemy from pushing between the Allies ; or, above all, that Napoleon was not responsible that Grouchy lost sight of the Prussians on the 17th ; does so either because he seeks not for the truth, or because, being blinded by previous conviction of his hero's infallibility, he makes his search in vain. Since the Emperor will ever be the true hero of the drama, let us illustrate this in his person. To do so it is only necessary for us here, having traced his errors in detail, to glance at the 'Observations' which he bequeathed to the world at the close of his narrative in the Mémoires, in order to discover how he failed, on mature consideration years after, and in his last utterance on the subject, to justify his own conduct of the campaign.

These 'Observations,' which are delivered with the assumed tone of an impartial critic, are nine in number. The first replies to some charges as to his doubtful home policy at this era, and falls outside the purely military question. The second praises himself for the boldness and sagacity of his concentration and surprise of the Allies : but though just enough here in the general, the correspondence of Wellington and Blücher abundantly shows that he overrated his own secresy greatly when he says that his 'movements were concealed from the enemy's knowledge up to the opening of the campaign.' This was not the case, as has been shown. That he was allowed so fair a chance by the quiescence of the Allies in their cantonments must be ascribed rather to their over-confidence than to his own skill.

In his third 'Observation,' Napoleon begins with a general accusation of his lieutenants, whose characters he declares to have been deteriorated by circumstances. Hence, he says, came the delay twice caused by Vandamme's personal faults on the first day, which lost seven hours, and prevented the advance being

Mém. ix. 157.

Ibid. 158.

Ante, pp. 66, 67.

made as far as Fleurus, 'whither the design of the General-in-Chief had been to place his headquarters on this very day.' Now, it so happens that Grouchy has complained, in one of his pamphlets, of the second delay of Vandamme, and has thus provoked Thiers, anxious at each turn to prove the Marshal incorrect, to draw attention to the positive assertion of Napoleon in another part of the Mémoires, that he had no intention of going farther that day than the point where his troops halted. In thus exonerating Vandamme the national historian unconsciously illustrates the utterly untrustworthy nature of the records of St. Helena. Either Napoleon did intend to push farther on, and the reply to Rogniat in the eighth volume is false ; or else the delay of Vandamme was not, as stated in the ' Observation ' we are discussing, ' very unfortunate ' (' *bien fâcheuse* '), and this charge is an afterthought invented for a purpose. The rest of the third ' Observation ' relates to the alleged delays of Ney on the 16th and 17th, which have been already shown to be in the direct fulfilment of his master's orders.

Mém. ix. 159.

Thi. xx. 4, *n*. 3.

Mém. viii. 196.

Ante, p. 93, *n.*

Ante, pp. 111–115, 146–150 ; and Mém. ix. 161.

The fourth refers to the distrust entertained of their generals by the French soldiers. Bourmont's desertion is mentioned, and the loss of Waterloo attributed partly to the treacherous cry of *sauve qui peut* being raised. ' It is equally probable,' it is added, ' that several officers carrying orders disappeared.' This may indeed be equally probable : but as no writer of weight on either side appears to be impressed with the

worth of these alleged causes of the defeat, we may be
excused from discussing them here as of any serious
importance.

  The next deals with the two subjects of Grouchy's
march, and of the waste of cavalry at Waterloo. Of
the former, though admitting that the Marshal slept
at Gembloux and had to move on Wavre, the ex-
Emperor declares that he might have been at the
latter place at 6 a.m. instead of 4 p.m. It is sufficient here to observe that, starting after a good
rest, the column actually took $4\frac{1}{2}$ hours to reach
Nil St. Vincent, not quite halfway ! For the rest,
we may leave the question of the responsibility for
Grouchy's conduct as already discussed fully, and
fixed on the right shoulders. We may pass over
with it that of the murderous folly which threw the
cavalry away, remarking only that what Napoleon
terms ' an unfortunate accident ' (' *accident fâcheux* ')
would, by any other critic reviewing any other commander, be called unhesitatingly a disastrous blunder.
With this last accident or error Napoleon, in this
his latest version, couples his want of a chief of the
corps of Guards, mentioned in the former, feeling, as
it is fair to conclude, the necessity for every possible
excuse. Of this alleged want enough has been already said to show that it was effectively supplied.

  The remaining four ' Observations ' are animad-
versions upon the conduct of the Allied commanders.
They are criticised sharply for their want of information, their wrong measures in concentrating, and

Ante,
p. 178.
Ante, pp.
188–196.

Ante, pp.
197–198.

Mém. ix.
165.

Gourg.
p. 94.

See ante,
p. 198.

their mistakes in agreeing to the project of fighting at Waterloo, which involved a bad position for Wellington, and a doubt of Blücher's being up in time. They should have retired, Napoleon asserts, more together after the defeat of Ligny, and, if this were impossible, have united before Brussels instead of at the point selected. Mém. ix. 166.

If these reflections, which are given at much length, have any weight, they serve but to condemn more deeply the writer, who, against enemies that offered him such opportunities, so miserably failed.

To confute this defence, or any founded (as it, after all, is mainly) upon the conduct of Grouchy, it is necessary only to study the facts as they really occurred, divesting oneself of any prepossession for or against Napoleon ; and the truth stands clearly out. Not to use the results of the new school of French critics, such as Charras, who may be supposed hostile to the Emperor's fame, let us select, from the historians of the other three nations concerned, a single representative writer, as dispassionate in his views as can be found, and trace the identity of their general views as to the reality of the blunder made in the wide and late pursuit prescribed to the Marshal.

' It is perfectly clear,' says Kennedy, ' that Napoleon acted under two erroneous impressions ; for, first, he had no idea that the whole Prussian army was to be put in motion against him from Wavre on the morning of the 18th ; and, second, he had Kenn. p. 163.

the full and confident conviction that he was strong
enough with the army he had with him to defeat and
destroy that of Wellington. . . . As to this second
alleged error, it may be said that it has not been
proved that he was wrong in supposing that he would
have defeated Wellington, had Wellington not been
supported by the Prussians.   But this does not mate-
rially affect the question, it having been clearly proved
that, even had the result been ultimately favourable to
Napoleon, the struggle would have been so desperate,
and the loss on both sides so enormous, that *Napoleon's
calculation was erroneous in not having brought
against Wellington every man and horse* that it was
possible for him to collect.'

Ante,
p. 195.
Kennedy is here speaking of the Emperor's approving Grouchy's continued movement on Wavre, by
his letter written just before the battle began ; and the
argument seems completely unanswerable.   It is clear
that he knew nothing of the Prussian flank march ; it
is no less clear that he felt certain of being able to dis-
pense with Grouchy.   His strategy was, therefore,
faulty in two vital points.

This judgment was delivered after nearly half a
century's light had been shed upon the subject, yet,
in the essential part, it agrees with that of Müffling,
in the earliest criticism worth quoting ever published
on the campaign.   Speaking of the supposed flank
movement of Grouchy to try and intercept the Prus-
Müff. Hist.
p. 69.
sians, this author says, ' This would no longer have
been of any avail, because at all events Marshal

Grouchy could not have arrived until after the battle was decided. *His faults on the* 17th *were so great that it was no longer possible on the* 18th *to make up for them.*' When he wrote this, but a few months after the events, it is clear that the historian gave credit to the current French story, that Grouchy's wrong direction to Gembloux and his late march on the 17th were of his own choice. It has been shown that *these mistakes were not his but Napoleon's* ; and the inference from this opinion also is unavoidable, that it was Napoleon who had thrown Grouchy beyond all available distance on the day of the battle.

Müff. Hist. p. 62.

Ante, p. 154, &c.

To turn to the Belgian critic Brialmont, who is more generally favourable to Napoleon than the English or Prussian one, and who assumes in his narrative the authenticity of the apocryphal night dispatches to Grouchy, we find his summary of the question as between the Emperor and Marshal to be as follows :—

' The faults charged on Grouchy are certainly very grave ; but impartial judges have given their opinion, that if this Marshal had received precise instructions, and if all the necessary precautions had been taken to cause the orders sent in the night of the 17th and on the morning of the 18th to reach him, he would have been upon the field of battle in time.' After looking into the question of the effect of his coming up, this author gives his opinion that, unless Grouchy had had the courage to march direct on the Prussian flank at St. Lambert, his resolve to join the Emperor could

Brial. ii. p. 433.

Brial. ii.
434.
have produced no great result. ' To sum up : he did no wrong to the French army, save in that he did not at this juncture prove to be a great captain.' But it is not necessary to follow the criticism so far as this, inasmuch as it has been proved that, by all the rules of

Ante,
p. 159.
evidence, the two orders Brialmont refers to must be rejected from history as inventions ; and this done, the opinion of the Belgian, like that of the English and Prussian writers, completely absolves the Marshal, and, in doing so, condemns Napoleon.

In the work of the great advocate of Napoleon's fame there is a remarkable passage, which confirms the impression drawn from a study of the facts and the opinion of impartial judges ; for it shows Thiers dissatisfied at heart with his own defence of the military idol of his nation, and willing finally to sacrifice the political and moral reputation of Napoleon to save his name for infallibility as a general. After reviewing his own arguments as to the conduct of Grouchy, he proceeds thus to enlarge upon the relation of this to the master who made Grouchy what he was :—

Thi. xx.
294.
' Thus his forgetfulness [Grouchy's] of his proper part, which was to separate the Prussians from the English, was the true cause of our misfortunes. We are speaking of the material cause ; for the moral cause we must look higher, and here Napoleon appears the real culprit.

' If you regard this four-days' campaign in its highest aspect, you will see not actual faults of the

Captain (who had never been more profound, more active, more full of resource), but those of the Head of the State, who had created for himself and for France a strained situation, where nothing went on naturally, and where the most powerful genius must fail before insurmountable moral obstacles. Surely nothing could be finer or more able than his combinations [at the opening]. . . . But the hesitation of Ney and Reille on the 15th, renewed upon the 16th, which rendered incomplete a success that should have been decisive, may be charged upon Napoleon, since it was he who had graven on their minds the memories which so powerfully affected them. . . . The loss of time on the 17th again was due to Ney's hesitation for half the day, to a storm for the other half. This storm was not the act of Napoleon, nor of his lieutenants : but it was his act that placed him in a situation where the least physical accident became a grave danger ; where, in order to escape destruction, it was necessary to have all the circumstances favourable without any exception, a thing which nature never grants to any captain.

'Again on the 18th, . . . if Reille was discouraged before Hougoumont, if Ney, if D'Erlon, after the fever-fit of hesitation of the 16th, had one of excitement on the 18th, and spent our most precious forces before the right moment—we repeat it here again—on Napoleon, who placed them in situations so strange, is to be charged the cause of their moral state, of this vast but ill-judged heroism. . . . So the fault of turning his attention from the centre, when such grave faults were committed, to the right, lay in the arrival of the Prussians, due to Grouchy alone, whatever may be said of it. But the fault of having Grouchy there—this fault so great—was Napoleon's own, who, to recompense political services, had chosen a man brave and loyal beyond doubt, but incapable of managing an army under such circumstances. . . . And to omit nothing in concluding, the feverish state of the army, which from the sublime of heroism fell into an unheard-of panic, was like all the rest the work of the Chief of the State, who during a reign of fifteen years had misused everything—France, army, genius—all that God had placed in his prodigal hands !'

Such is Thiers's final defence of his ideal general. Such the summing-up of a judgment, to support which it is necessary, as has been shown at some length, to pervert testimony, to misquote Napoleon's own writings, to blacken honourable names, and to ignore all facts conflicting with the favoured theory. And when the object is gained, and a great nation persuaded of the invincibility—but for accident—of its chosen general ; is the legacy of restless ambition Napoleon bequeathed so precious that he deserves this apotheosis at the historian's hands ? Does the historian himself merit national honour and the Academic prize, who has bestowed on his country a gift so rife with future evil as the sparkling poison of ' The Consulate and Empire ' ?

In the preceding portion of these lectures it has been intended mainly to follow the facts as they occurred. Our criticisms of Napoleon have been founded naturally upon them, since most writers take it for granted that his design throughout was as able as daring, and reason on it accordingly. Indeed, the Ante, p. 50, &c. common consent of all critics, excepting Wellington alone, agrees that the plan of the advance through Charleroi, and of a division of, and separate attack on, the Allies, was the best hope of success for the French. Wellington, we know, took a different view Sup. Disp. p. 522,525. in his Memorandum of 1842 ; but the inaccuracies already referred to as patent in that paper, and the Ante, pp. 79, 123, 153. fact of his argument as to Napoleon's advance being but part of a defence of his own conduct in looking more to his right than to the point really threatened, deprive his opinion of that weight which would otherwise attach to it. It is hardly too much to say, therefore, that it may be unhesitatingly accepted that Napoleon could not have opened his campaign, under the circumstances, on a better method than he did.

Its faults in execution ; the feebleness and hesitation with which his movements on the following morning began ; the utter want of insight into the real state of the Prussians and of the Allied plan, which he showed after his success at Ligny ; have been fully shown in our preceding pages. But a greater error than lies in such details has been charged upon him by certain writers of authority ; and we should not be completing our task satisfactorily if we failed to bring to notice their views on this most important question of strategy.

It is evident that, after the defeat of Blücher, there were three courses open to Napoleon for the prosecution of his campaign. The first, and apparently the simplest, was *to follow the retreating enemy at once with the troops in hand*, and to endeavour to obtain as much advantage as possible by a vigorous pursuit, leaving Ney to check Wellington for the time. The second, *to turn away* from the Prussians altogether, *and, uniting with Ney, throw his entire force against Wellington.* The third was *the medium plan* which the Emperor adopted, and which we need not here discuss, save in its relation to the others.

To consider the second : Was it absolutely necessary for Napoleon to make the large detachment under Grouchy, which left his numbers inferior to Wellington's ? Was it even advisable thus to diminish his means of crushing the English general ? Such are the questions which suggest themselves, and to which Thiers has undertaken to make a special reply in his final summary of the campaign. As the pith of his argument is not lengthy, it is best given in the author's words, who here seeks a new opportunity of vehement reproach of Grouchy : ' Ah ! doubtless, if you suppose in the command of our right wing a blindness unparalleled in history, a blindness such as to allow 80,000 Prussians to do as they liked before it, and even to overwhelm Napoleon, lately their victor,

Thi. xx. 280.

without opposition, there will be reason to say that
this detachment of the right wing was a fault.' Following out this distinct admission, and a remarkable
one made in the next paragraph—where, speaking
of the instructions given Grouchy, the author says,
' there may, doubtless, be differences of opinion as to
their exact meaning ' (' on peut sans doute disputer sur
leur signification ')—it follows clearly, on the showing
of the latest and ablest of Napoleon's advocates, that
it was an error of the Emperor to make the detachment of Grouchy at all, supposing it possible for the
Marshal to act as he actually did. Thiers thinks it
not possible that this could have been foreseen : but
to those who take a different view of Napoleon—who
prefer the judgment of the historian to the opinion
of the advocate—to such the mistake will appear very
possible, were it only from the fact that the event so
difficult to foresee did actually occur. Having quoted
what Thiers has said in defence of the detachment of
Grouchy, let us place near it the condemnation in the
words of Kennedy—a critic who will not be accused,
by those who know his work, of any desire to deal
more hardly with the great French captain than with
his opponents. After an examination of Napoleon's
defence of himself on this point (which is founded on Gourg.
the necessity of guarding against a possible rally of the p. 95.
Prussians, followed by an advance on Fleurus to seize
his communications), and after showing, in careful
detail, that no such contingency should have affected Kenn. p.
the immediate object, the attack of Wellington's still 155, 158.

R

disunited forces, Kennedy goes on to say, in an argument which deserves the attentive study of those who would view the broad features of the campaign in their true light :

' But the assertion that Napoleon's dividing his army was a vast error, is founded upon higher and more important considerations. On the morning of the 17th of June he was operating with about 100,000 men against about 200,000 men ; and it was manifestly and absolutely essential to him, in the military and political position in which he stood, to defeat, separate, and paralyse the armies of Wellington and Blücher, in order that he might have even the least chance of re-establishing himself on the throne of France.

' His great difficulty, as he ought well to have known, from the experience of a whole succession of disastrous campaigns to his armies in Spain, was the overthrow of the Anglo-Allied army ; and against it he should have led his last man and horse, even had the risk been great in the highest degree—which, as has been seen, it clearly was not. Had Napoleon attacked the Anglo-Allied army with his whole force and succeeded in defeating it, there could be little question of his being able to defeat afterwards the Prussian army, when separated from Wellington's ; so that, of all suppositions, the most favourable to Napoleon's ultimate success would be that of the Prussian army having attempted to intercept his line of communication : yet it is upon this fallacious argu-

ment that Napoleon—with at least an assumed sin-
cerity—justifies so confidently the division of his force.
It will appear to most minds too bold to say that
Napoleon took a view of his case and position below
what the circumstances called for. That the man
who had, by his genius and energy and the vastness
of his views, gone far towards the conquest of all
Europe, should have failed to play a great game in a
case on which his whole fortunes hinged, is certainly
difficult to understand : but it must be borne in mind
that there is a distinction between vastness of views
and the personal conduct of operations ; and that it is
not at all inconsistent with sound views to suppose
that, while a man was rising to power, and throwing
for empire first and then for conquest, he might be
more fitted for playing a desperate game than when
acting a more defensive part at a more advanced
period of his career. It was necessary that Napoleon,
under the circumstances, should throw for entire
success, and he failed to do so : this was acting a part
incommensurate with the circumstances in which he
was placed ; for anything short of complete success
would have entailed his ruin as certainly as a defeat
would have done. He failed, therefore, in not playing
a great enough game.'

Even those who refuse to accede to this opinion will
possibly, on consideration, admit that it requires a
better answer than is to be found in the works of
Napoleon or his admirers. The bolder course which
Kennedy speaks of, cannot at any rate be termed the

mere afterthought of a theorist, when it is known that it was suggested on the spot to the Emperor by the very man who was compelled to carry out the weaker plan which his master chose. If Grouchy's word be worth anything, that unfortunate officer, amid the remonstrances which he offered on the 17th against a regular pursuit of the Prussians, then far out of sight, did actually propose as an alternative,* that a division of 10,000 strong only should be charged with their observation, and *that he himself, with all the rest of the Ligny troops, should co-operate in the movement to be made by Ney's wing against Wellington.* Napoleon, as is well known, rebuked his lieutenant for his nervousness, and bade him go at once to his new duty. For in his later years, as in those of his prosperity, he seldom cared to take the opinion of others on his plans, and, even when listening to it, followed his own counsel.

Thi. xx. 156.

As at Mantua in 1796, Thi. Rév. viii. 278; and after Aspern in 1809. Thi. x. 335.

If there are any still incredulous of the possibility of this great general's choosing the wrong course after Ligny, we invite them to consider what is said on the subject by Clausewitz, at once the most practical and the most philosophic of all military critics. As Kennedy has given especial proofs that, in detaching

---

* This singular fact, hitherto unpublished, has reached the author through the kindness of Lord de Ros. It rests on the authority of Mr. Hughes, formerly American Minister at the Hague, who heard it from the Marshal soon after his arrival in the United States, when the facts of the campaign were fresh in his memory. The coincidence of the original suggestion with Kennedy's theoretical view is too striking to be passed over.

Grouchy, Napoleon took a weaker course than in throwing his whole force on Wellington, so the great Prussian writer has devoted a chapter to the consideration of the third choice open to Napoleon after Ligny. This he very properly terms a chief strategical question of the campaign, and commences his inquiry by defining its object thus :—' Would not Napoleon have done better to pursue Blücher on the 17th with his main army, and either by the mere operation of a very energetic pursuit to have brought him into a sort of confused rout, and so driven him over the Meuse, or in case Blücher ventured on a second battle that day or the following, inflicted on him a decisive defeat ? '

The answer to this is given with the author's usual skill and elaborate care. The original must be referred to for a study of it in full details. It is sufficient here to say that Clausewitz appears clearly in the right when he asserts that Napoleon, on the 17th, had just as much power of bringing Blücher to a second battle as he had of compelling Wellington to deliver one, and that the moral consequences of a second victory over the already defeated enemy would have enhanced vastly the result of Ligny ; whereas, if Blücher had escaped by continuing his retreat precipitately, Napoleon, by a vigorous pursuit, would have reaped enough indemnity to repay himself for the disappointment, and would still have been able to turn against Wellington. Supposing, it is added, the latter had pressed Ney, left alone in his front, and

Claus. p. 175.

had even beaten him and driven him over the Sambre, the Emperor could have afforded the loss of 40,000 men to put 115,000 enemies out of his way for the time.   True it is that his victory over Blücher would have been less sure than Wellington's over Ney : but, on the other hand, Napoleon was in a situation that required a risk in order to win, and should have laid excessive caution aside.   From such caution, from useless delays, from pursuing Blücher, when he did at last pursue him, with an inferior force, it came about that the Prussians obtained time to collect

Claus. p. 180.

and rally their troops anew.   ' Had Napoleon pursued at once with his main army, he might have offered battle early on the 18th at Wavre.   It is very doubtful whether Blücher ' [it is from a chief actor on the Prussian Staff we are quoting, as well as from a great critic] ' was in a condition to have accepted it at that place and time, and it is still more so whether Wellington could have got up in good time to aid him.'   Probably Napoleon erred from underrating his enemy's power of rallying, being led away by remembrances of earlier victories ; but at any rate he did err in the opinion of his critic.   The change of direction which, at this point, he gave to his main army, damaged the whole working of the campaign, and was (as in 1813, when he so acted after Dresden, and in 1814 after Montmirail) both theoretically and practically a complete mistake, if Clausewitz be right.

Summary of the Campaign.

To revert finally from possibilities to the actual events of which we have now finished our review. Those who have regarded them with us dispassionately, and in their aspect as a whole, will perceive in this great drama of war a unity and completeness which many writers on the campaign have missed. Stripped of superfluous ornament, and of the mass of fiction wherewith national vanity has obscured it, the story of Waterloo becomes clear and simple enough. On the one side is an army taking the offensive under the most renowned leader of the world, itself formidable by tradition, training, and devotion to its chief ; compact in organisation, and complete in all its parts, moving by the volition of a single will, and with the political circumstances subordinated to the military, it must be regarded as the most formidable instrument of war which the age could produce. Opposed stand two Allies, each commanding a force nearly equal to the French, each honoured and trusted by his soldiers, but each aware that the composition of his troops was inferior to that of the foe. Faithful co-operation to the common end was their reliance to maintain the superiority promised by their numbers : meanwhile, for conveniency's sake, their armies lie scattered over a front of more than 100 miles, and that, although they knew the enemy to be threatening a decisive blow. He advances with a sudden spring across the frontier, aiming straight at the point where their cantonments meet upon his shortest road to Brussels ; his speed and earnestness show his resolve to be either to thrust his army between them, or to strike a deadly blow at him who should most quickly gather for the encounter. The Allies have provided beforehand, in their counsels, for this very case, resolved to fight side by side, the one ready to support the other ; but Napoleon's prompt advance anticipates their design, and on the first day the mass of his army is upon the ground laid out for their junction, whilst Blücher can only gain its vicinity next morning with three-fourths of his force, and Wellington with a mere fraction of the British. The second day finds the Allied commanders in personal council at Ligny, whilst Napoleon prepares to thrust the Prussians out of his way. Wellington promises them his support, being unaware that Napoleon has placed a strong left wing before the British, as though anticipating the attempt to unite on this new line.

Attacked by Ney, the British commander has full occupation for the rest of the day, and, though successful himself, can furnish no succour to Blücher, who suffers a sharp defeat. Thus far matters seem to have prospered with Napoleon, but from this night his star of destiny wanes sensibly each hour. Whilst the Allies, firm to their original resolve, fall back on the 17th on lines as nearly parallel as the circumstances permit, to seek a new point of junction at Waterloo, he overrates his own advantage, mistakes

the direction of retreat taken by the Prussians, and
instead of following hotly from early daylight on their
track, or marching instantly with all his force on
Wellington's flank, he loses half the day before his
decision is made, and then takes the intermediate
measure of sending a large detachment after the
Prussians, and of following Wellington with the rest.
From this hour his fate is sealed ; for complete and
sudden victory, his one hope of safety from threatened
ruin, has become henceforth impossible. Calm in
the coming certainty of success, the British general,
without even calling in all troops available for the
battle, turns to face his renowned adversary at the
chosen post of Waterloo, where cross-roads from
Blücher's rallying-point at Wavre afford the means
of the union twice before prevented. Napoleon, on
the morning of the 18th, remains utterly ignorant
of their design, believing the army before him the
only obstacle to his entry into Brussels, and the
Prussians still retreating before Grouchy. If any part
of their dispersed force has gone to Wavre, as is
reported, Grouchy can push it off with ease, and is
directed that way. The momentous battle is deferred
from hour to hour until the ground shall be con-
veniently dry, and the magnificent array of the French
be displayed fully to the enemy in all its imposing
proportions. This ruinous delay, which proves him
so ignorant of his true danger, brings the Prussians,
though slow at first, within sight of his flank before

the battle is well opened; and the terrible truth
bursts upon him. With hot-headed courage, but
ill-judged tactics, his lieutenants make a series of
attacks, which once only, and that for a brief space,
shake the firm line of Wellington : but the British
leader owes to the first appearance of Blücher the advantage that the Emperor strips himself of the greater
part of his formidable reserves. Meanwhile the intended junction of the Allies draws on, and detailed
arrangements of the most exact kind are made to
ensure that the co-operation of the Prussians may be
the most effective possible. Grouchy, following them
steadily but slowly, refuses to turn aside from his line
of march to the distant firing, since he knows that the
Emperor had not counted on him for the battle with
Wellington, and that his task is solely with the Prussians, whom he believes still to be near Wavre. Here
he finds and attacks their rear-guard; but Blücher,
with glorious hardihood, leaves it to its fate, caring
only for what is to be done in front of Waterloo.
His troops once fairly on the fatal ground, the object
of the campaign on the part of the Allies is at last
accomplished, and a victory, complete beyond all
precedent, rewards their combination. The strategy
to which Napoleon had looked to atone, as in his early
glories, for inferiority of numbers, fails him utterly in
face of the firm compact and mutual trust of Wellington and Blücher. The sword to which he loved
to appeal is stricken from his grasp for ever. Henceforth a lonely exile, he lives only to brood over his

mighty past, to paint his mistakes as calamities, his fall as the work of others ; consoled, it may be, by a vision of the day when a meretricious romance, based on his own figments, shall be accepted by the French for their national history.

THE NAPOLEONIC LIBRARY

Other books in the series include:

FROM CORUNNA TO WATERLOO
The Letters and Journals of Two Napoleonic Hussars
1801–1816
Edited by Gareth Glover

ON THE FIELDS OF GLORY
The Battlefields of the 1815 Campaign
Andrew Uffindell and Michael Corum

LIFE IN NAPOLEON'S ARMY
The Memoirs of Captain Elzéar Blaze
Introduction by Philip Haythornthwaite

THE MEMOIRS OF BARON VON MÜFFLING
A Prussian Officer in the Napoleonic Wars
Baron von Müffling

WATERLOO LECTURES
A Study of the Campaign of 1815
Colonel Charles Chesney

WATERLOO LETTERS
A Collection of Accounts From Survivors
of the Campaign of 1815
Edited by Major-General H. T. Siborne

www.frontline-books.com/napoleoniclibrary